FOREWORD

Defining what is art and what makes an artist, especially in the 21st century, is no easy feat. In the late 19th century Oscar Wilde poetically attempted to answer these questions in the preface to his novel 'The Picture of Dorian Grey.' As part of his examination, he stated: "The artist is the creator of beautiful things...The artist can express everything...All art is quite useless."

Despite Wilde's arguably accurate assertions, it is necessary to continuously re-examine and redefine the meaning of art and of the artist. As the technological age in which we live shows no signs of slowing, new forms of potential art continuously present themselves and with every pre, post and current 'ism' affecting, creating and hindering new artistic forms, there is more work to be considered than ever. Is the magnificence of a starry night in a new video game the modern equivalent to a Van Gogh? Should your sleek and dynamic smartphone be the subject of songs? Will the sound of sports cars echo louder through the ages than the sound of poetry? Quite possibly.

CAN BRICKS BE CONSIDERED ART?

Where there is form there is the potential for art to be perceived. As technology continues to provide new and accessible ways to explore artistic expression, the ever-changing face of art is becoming more abstract and appearing in some of the most unlikely of places. Whether it be cave paintings, marble statues, tapestries, books, paintings, monuments, photographs, films, video games – or LEGO creations – each have a story to tell and a place to be appreciated.

This story is about Chicago-born multi-medium artist Adam Reed Tucker, whose work breaks boundaries by blending architecture and sculpture. In the traditional senses of the words, architecture is the process of designing and constructing buildings; sculpture is the production of a two or three-dimensional shape from static material. However, there is no clay, nor is there wood, glue or metal in his work; Adam's preferred medium is the humble and universally-recognized LEGO brick. Favored for eliminating the need for tools and glue, it's Adam's belief that LEGO bricks level the playing field and allow the individual to instantly focus on expressing their creativity. Only his story can explain how this philosophy came to be. It is an inspirational story of a man who developed his passion for his childhood's construction toys into a career as a qualified architect, then unleashed the potential of LEGO bricks on the world to become a recognized professional artist.

Almost every child has access to LEGO bricks and all of those children have the potential to create art. This is the story of one of those children.

Adam with his supportive family: Brittny, his wife, and son Jaxson all embracing Goofy.

Adam's dog Morgan can either be found hiding behind his creations or checking on each build's progress, often with brick in mouth.

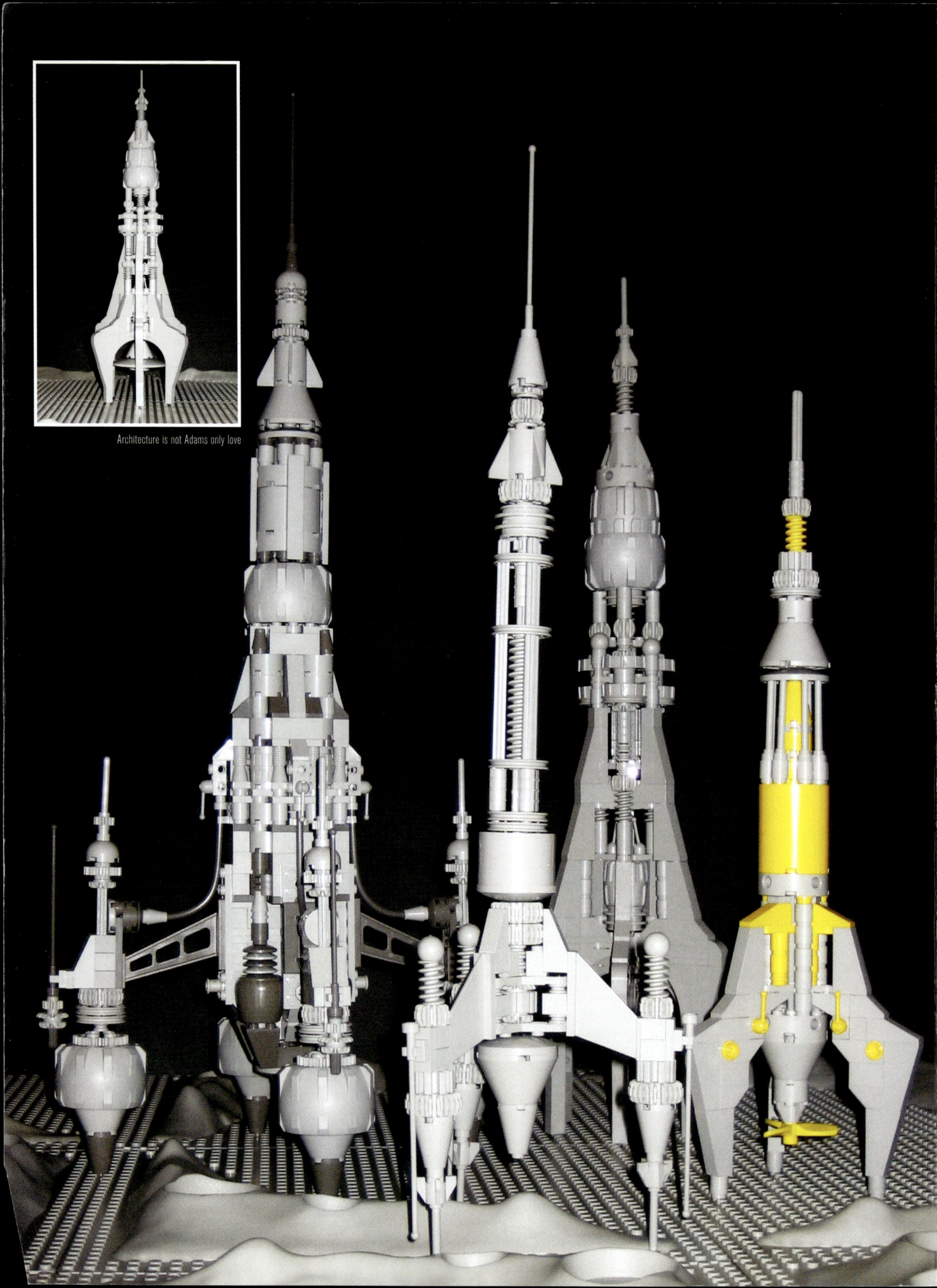

Architecture is not Adams only love

CONTENTS

3 FOREWORD
Can bricks be considered art?

8 EMBRACING CREATIVITY
The early life of Adam Reed Tucker, and how his parents' artistic outlook shaped his childhood.

14 GOING AWAY TO COLLEGE
How the young artist began to develop the academic theory embedded within his work.

24 LIGHT AT THE END
Adam's return to the brick after the introduction of the Star Wars LEGO theme.

28 THE PROFESSIONAL YEARS
A successful career as an architect leads to a pivotal question.

34 THE LIGHT BULB MOMENT
The realization that LEGO bricks could be incorporated back into the artist's life.

38 HOUSE OF BRICKS - CHICAGO
The artist's first test to see if his own kits held appeal with LEGO fans.

44 BRICKFEST WASHINGTON
After traveling 700 miles Adam puts his kits into the hands of The LEGO Group.

46 THE BEGINNING OF ARCHITECTURE
A quick look at the origins of BrickStructures that unbeknownst then would be the foundations of the architecture theme.

48 GETTING CERTIFIED - THE 7TH MEMBER
To secure the talents of the artist, The LEGO Group invite Adam to join the elite LEGO Certified Professional program.

54 BUILDING A NEW RELATIONSHIP
A series of chance taking and maverick ideas leads to the creation and fulfilment of the LEGO Architecture range.

64 CREATING EVENTS
How a gruelling 700-mile drive in an un-air-conditioned van led to the development of the hit Chicago LEGO show: Brickworld.

66 GOING BEYOND
Going from strength to strength, Adam creates a touring exhibition of LEGO models to inspire others to build.

76 ARCHITECTURE - CREATING A NEW EXPERIENCE
The range, as created by Adam, displayed in all their glory.

86 A LEGO EDUCATION
As Adam's name and his creative values is resonated throughout The LEGO Group, the artist becomes the keynote speaker at the LEGO Education summit.

90 MASTER BUILDER ACADEMY
The release of the beautiful 20215 Invention Designer, and the untimely demise of Master Builder Academy.

96 THE WORK OF ADAM REED TUCKER
The artist's privately commissioned collection.

102 A VISUAL GUIDE
A look at the beautiful DK books guide to LEGO Architecture.

106 A MOMENT IN THE LIMELIGHT
How the hit LEGO Brickumentary put the artist in the limelight.

108 BRICK BY BRICK
After the success of his touring exhibition, Adam puts on his biggest display yet.

134 CONSIDERING THE CLASSICS
Turning the attention to the sets that hold Adam's favor.

138 EPILOGUE - BRICK THEORY
Why Adam uses the brick as a Medium.

Editor-in-chief: Mark Guest
Features editor: Lewis Matthews
Sub editor: Caroline Schmidt
Pictures copyright: Adam Reed Tucker, Andrew Tipping, The LEGO group 2017© BRICK BY BRICK Photo Credits: ©2017 J.B. Spector / Museum of Science and Industry, Chicago
Printed by: Matrix Print

ADAM REED TUCKER PROFESSIONAL HIGHLIGHTS

KSU GRADUATION: 5-YEAR PROFESSIONAL BACHELOR DEGREE IN ARCHITECTURE 1996

BRICKSTRUCTURES, INC., FOUNDED 2006
Left Architecture Practice 2007
Became an LCP 2007
Founded Brickworld June 2007

BEGAN WORKING WITH TLG ON LEGO ARCHITECTURE 2007-2008
LEGO Architecture Test Sets 2007
Sears Tower
John Hancock Center

Looptopia, Chicago Architecture Foundation, exhibitor 2008

Special Guest Appearance - Lego Architecture, Legoland Burj Khalifa build 2008

Science Chicago - 2009
St. Louis Science Center - St. Louis Arch model display 2009
I-Hobby Expo - featured exhibitor 2009

2010 - Wired, Best Innovation

2009 - Wallpaper*, Best Design

LEGO Architecture Award
LEGO Architecture Award

Timeline: 1996 1997 1998 1999 2000 2001 2002 2003 2004 2005 2006 2007 2008 2009 2010

Kansas City 1997-2000
Chicago 2000-2006
YEARS WORKING AS AN ARCHITECT

STARTED EXPLORING ART AND DESIGN WITH THE LEGO BRICK 2005

Chicago House of Bricks May 2006
Brickfest August 2006

Skydeck Chicago - Sears Tower Big Build event 2008
Where University, Hospitality Convention, featured exhibitor 2008

Art of Architecture, Discovery Center Museum, Rockford, IL: October 2008 - December 2008

Art + Science = Architecture, Museum of Science and Industry, Chicago, IL July 2009 – March 2010

Lego Kidsfest, exhibit coordinator 2010

Sets Designed:
Sears Tower/Willis Tower (2011 re-launch)
John Hancock Center
Seattle Space Needle
Empire State Building
Guggenheim Museum
Fallingwater
Burj Khalifa
The White House
Robie House
Brandenburg Gate
Rockefeller Center
Farnsworth House
Sungnyemun Gate
Sydney Opera House
Leaning Tower of Pisa

LEGO ARCHITECTURE LAUNCH 2008

6 BRICKSCULTURE

Timeline

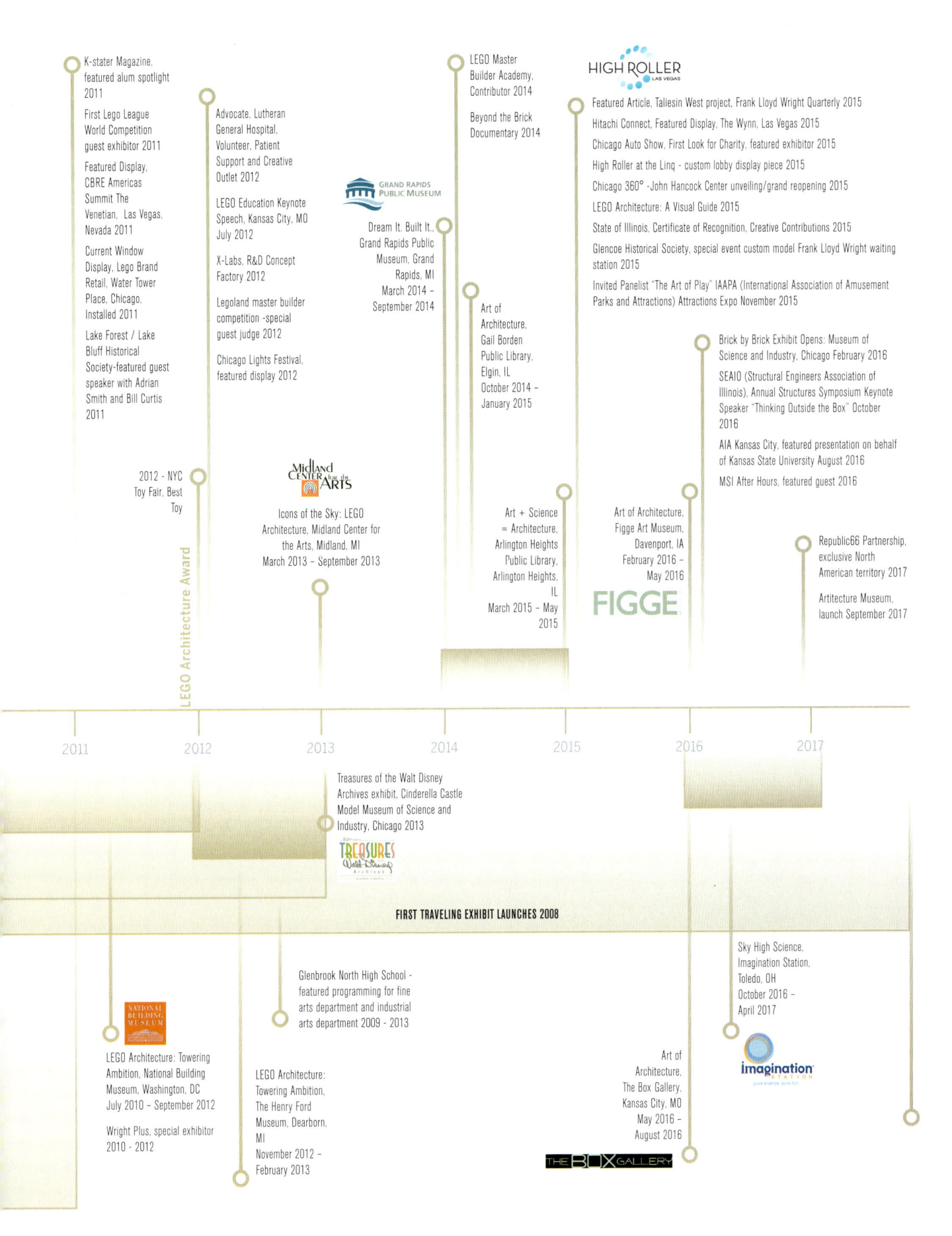

2011
- K-stater Magazine, featured alum spotlight 2011
- First Lego League World Competition guest exhibitor 2011
- Featured Display, CBRE Americas Summit The Venetian, Las Vegas, Nevada 2011
- Current Window Display, Lego Brand Retail, Water Tower Place, Chicago, Installed 2011
- Lake Forest / Lake Bluff Historical Society-featured guest speaker with Adrian Smith and Bill Curtis 2011

2012
- 2012 – NYC Toy Fair, Best Toy — LEGO Architecture Award
- Advocate, Lutheran General Hospital, Volunteer, Patient Support and Creative Outlet 2012
- LEGO Education Keynote Speech, Kansas City, MO July 2012
- X-Labs, R&D Concept Factory 2012
- Legoland master builder competition - special guest judge 2012
- Chicago Lights Festival, featured display 2012

2013
- Icons of the Sky: LEGO Architecture, Midland Center for the Arts, Midland, MI March 2013 – September 2013

2014
- LEGO Master Builder Academy, Contributor 2014
- Beyond the Brick Documentary 2014
- Dream It. Built It., Grand Rapids Public Museum, Grand Rapids, MI March 2014 – September 2014
- Art of Architecture, Gail Borden Public Library, Elgin, IL October 2014 – January 2015

2015
- Featured Article, Taliesin West project, Frank Lloyd Wright Quarterly 2015
- Hitachi Connect, Featured Display, The Wynn, Las Vegas 2015
- Chicago Auto Show, First Look for Charity, featured exhibitor 2015
- High Roller at the Linq - custom lobby display piece 2015
- Chicago 360° - John Hancock Center unveiling/grand reopening 2015
- LEGO Architecture: A Visual Guide 2015
- State of Illinois, Certificate of Recognition, Creative Contributions 2015
- Glencoe Historical Society, special event custom model Frank Lloyd Wright waiting station 2015
- Invited Panelist "The Art of Play" IAAPA (International Association of Amusement Parks and Attractions) Attractions Expo November 2015
- Art + Science = Architecture, Arlington Heights Public Library, Arlington Heights, IL March 2015 – May 2015

2016
- Brick by Brick Exhibit Opens: Museum of Science and Industry, Chicago February 2016
- SEAIO (Structural Engineers Association of Illinois), Annual Structures Symposium Keynote Speaker "Thinking Outside the Box" October
- AIA Kansas City, featured presentation on behalf of Kansas State University August 2016
- MSI After Hours, featured guest 2016
- Art of Architecture, Figge Art Museum, Davenport, IA February 2016 – May 2016

2017
- Republic66 Partnership, exclusive North American territory 2017
- Artiteture Museum, launch September 2017

FIRST TRAVELING EXHIBIT LAUNCHES 2008

- Treasures of the Walt Disney Archives exhibit, Cinderella Castle Model Museum of Science and Industry, Chicago 2013

- LEGO Architecture: Towering Ambition, National Building Museum, Washington, DC July 2010 – September 2012
- Wright Plus, special exhibitor 2010 - 2012

- Glenbrook North High School - featured programming for fine arts department and industrial arts department 2009 - 2013
- LEGO Architecture: Towering Ambition, The Henry Ford Museum, Dearborn, MI November 2012 – February 2013

- Art of Architecture, The Box Gallery, Kansas City, MO May 2016 – August 2016

- Sky High Science, Imagination Station, Toledo, OH October 2016 – April 2017

| THE EARLY YEARS

EMBRACING CREATIVITY

Dive into the early life of Adam Reed Tucker, learn how his parents' artistic outlook shaped his childhood, and the catalyst that started his amazing journey into the artistic world of LEGO construction

Artistic creativity is not a trait that can be taught, nor is there a standardized process for which children or adults can follow in order to gain a fundamental understanding of how to be creative. By the same token, creativity is not a binary dichotomy where people are either creative or not. Everyone has the ability to create and express their imaginative ideas whether it is by finger painting, dancing or solving problems. If we all possess the ability to be creative, then the main question is: How does one become enlightened to your own personal creativity in order to utilise it? More so, at what point can you start to weave your thoughts into actions and express yourself in a way that is deemed to be creative? These were the questions that the Tuckers' considered upon the birth of their son Adam, in the northern suburbs of Chicago on 1 November 1971. Their desire was not to raise a child who was 'creative', but to nurture and inspire their son so that creativity was not just an ability but a constant way of thinking.

Adam was fortunate enough to have a mother who embraced practical creativity as an interior designer and artist, and a father who took a more traditional route into the field of graphic design, earning himself awards that elevated his professional recognition. Adam's artistic parents decided to dedicate themselves to their child by carefully nurturing the most creative environment they could by immersing him in creative stimulation and inspiration. From first breath to first steps, creativity was weaved into as many activities as possible so that it became the natural lens with which he viewed the world. Similar to many children across the world, Adam's first real exploration of his own creativity was through play. Christmas in the early 1970s was the perfect opportunity for his parents to surround him in stimulating construction toys such as wooden blocks and Lincoln Logs.

It was at the young age of four that Adam's life unknowingly changed forever when his parents graduated him from simple building toys and gifted him his first LEGO set. Left to his own devices with his new bricks, Adam soon became familiar with the clicks and snaps that would fill his life with endless possibility. Immediately he was building almost perfect replicas of the models depicted on the box without even opening the instructions. This quickly caught the attention of his parents who, keen to explore this newfound skill and foster his creativity,

An early photograph (1978) of Adam modifying his mobile crane set 855A

|THE EARLY YEARS

Adam's artistic mother embraced LEGO bricks for their educational and creative value

continued gifting him classic 1970s sets such as the blue police station, released before the advent of the minifigure. It was the Tucker's belief that replicating the models of LEGO artwork was revealing, and improving upon, fundamental and tactile skills such as hand-eye coordination, color and shape recognition as well as problem solving. These skills are vital to expressing your imagination through art and so Adam's parents keenly set about encouraging building using LEGO bricks.

Adam recalls a childhood populated with 1970s system sets, which then developed into a liking for the Castle and Classic space themes popular in the 1980s. "Classic Space was my absolute favorite, Catalogue played a vital role in providing Adam with LEGO thematic inspiration. After meticulously studying the way the sets were constructed, Adam took to his old builds, tearing apart sets like his blue police station and re-engineering them with his newly-acquired techniques. These guides also began to make Adam question the realism of the color schemes. He began to realize that the LEGO models would not always share the colors of the real-life counterparts he saw in 1980s America, particularly the blue construction vehicles that in reality were yellow. Despite recognizing that the colors of official LEGO sets, and indeed his own builds, did not accurately represent the real-life, Adam chose to

"Classic Space was my absolute favourite, the first wave of classic space when the colour scheme was red and white"

especially the first wave of Classic Space when the color scheme was red and white. Later came the blue, yellow and black, but it was always the first wave that gripped me," exclaims Adam. It wasn't long before a trip to the Museum of Science and Industry in 1985 landed Adam with his first expert builder sets or, as Adam likes to call them, 'mechanical system sets'. That set was 1030 Simple Machines Technic set – an extensive set from the museum gift shop.

By this point Adam had disregarded the instructions entirely and at ten years old had taken to building the sets displayed on the box entirely from scratch, as well as free building from his imagination. Constantly looking for his own inspiration, the Technic Ideas focus on the structure of his builds and not to allow himself to be caught up with the need to build within the right color scheme – a vital skill that would be of benefit to him later in life. It was whilst thinking about these color problems that he came to realize that, in one way or another, when he grew up he would strive to work with The LEGO Group.

Most modern-day parents with little LEGO fans at home will have heard their child say "I want to be a LEGO designer when I grow up", but that usually comes after the classic roles of firefighter, doctor and police officer have been exhausted and new territories are being explored. As Adam, however, recalls it being his first choice: "I didn't know what

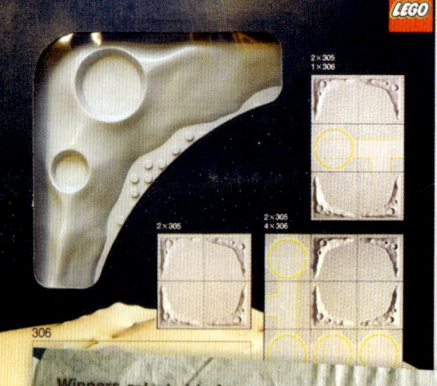

| THE EARLY YEARS

Classic Space proved to be one of Adam's favourite childhood themes, it still is to this day.

it meant, all I knew was that I wanted to work for The LEGO Group. Kids my age wanted normal jobs but all I knew was...I wanted to work for The LEGO Group!" This enthusiasm for LEGO remained within the young artist, even through the inception of other interests such as sports and girls – although building with LEGO bricks became more of a private passion during his early teenage years. The fear of ridicule and misunderstanding of Adam's hobby by his peers was not going to stop him from expressing his creativity, exploring and pushing the boundaries with his LEGO bricks – albeit from the privacy of his bedroom. By 15 years old, Adam was fully integrated into the normal sporting and social rights of passage expected of a child his age, but at home Adam had begun to take a more advanced and engineered approach to his LEGO hobby.

Captivated by gears and pulley systems, Adam began to see LEGO as more than just a tool to build extensions of his imagination; he started to see how it could recreate the mechanical and engineered world around him. This interest in mechanics lead to the exploration of other products such as Kenner's Girders and Panels, which enabled him to express his need for realism away from LEGO bricks. Adam began to learn how to create realistic structures because, unlike LEGO bricks, Girders and Panels allowed you to create much more true-to-life buildings using beams, columns and curtain wall panels. Experimenting with this new medium allowed Adam to understand that although building with LEGO bricks was full of possibilities, there were also hindrances to be overcome.

Over the years, LEGO bricks had become much more than a construction play toy. Adam had been taking the bricks and using them as a medium to fashion an artistic representation of the world he saw around him. But that wouldn't be the case for much longer. Despite a growing knowledge and artistic understanding, at the age of 16, Adam's interests and enthusiasm for LEGO construction all began

"Kids my age wanted normal jobs but all I knew was... I wanted to work for The LEGO Group"

to change. Reality anchored Adam's life to revolve around the usual teen activities of schoolbooks, sports, cars, dating and socializing with friends. All his LEGO bricks were retired to the attic as Adam moved on to high school. Slowly but surely, through garage sales and giveaways, Adam's treasured LEGO sets made their way into the world to inspire other children to build. Fortunately for Adam, the LEGO bug merely laid dormant and despite entering his dark age, the lessons the bricks taught him would continue to inspire the way he perceived the world, his interaction with artistic mediums, and of course his ongoing creative thinking.

|COLLEGE YEARS

GOING AWAY TO COLLEGE

Explore how the young artist began to develop the academic theory embedded within his work

Despite leaving his LEGO bricks behind, they had played a huge role in sculpting and opening the young artist's mind to the possibility of a creative career. Even though Adam's high school years showed he had no desire to stop learning or creating, it was a slightly stunted start due to his distracted lack of focus. Although it can seem concerning, it is a trait commonly found in creative children.

"I was a bad student, I wasn't the kind of student who applied himself as much as he could. I did the minimum to get by," reflects Adam. Academically that was true for Adam, as it is for a lot of students. When Academia feels too detached from creativity it can be hard for students to find their focus in school, and can often lead to a lack of interest, poor grades and misbehavior. It is therefore paramount that young creatives are realized by teachers and not taught that science or math is important just because 'they are'. They need to understand that they are important because through the application of those disciplines, you can more successfully apply yourself to understanding and discovering your creative focus. After all, spending free time engaging in your own chosen activities leads to far more productivity than sitting in a silenced detention room.

Adam took a backseat to traditionally academic subjects and opted to dive right into the very center of creation, submersing

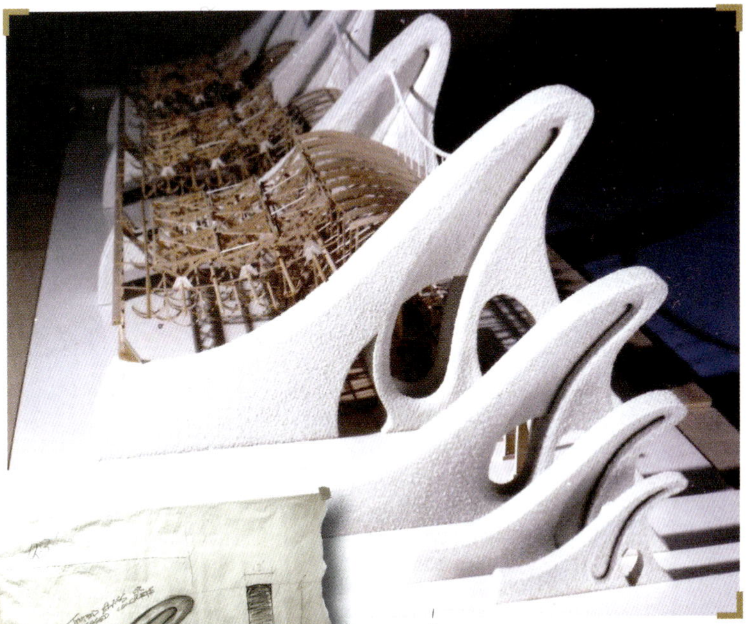

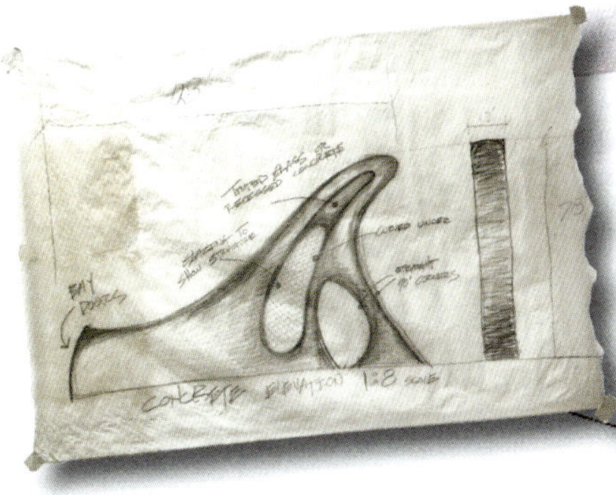

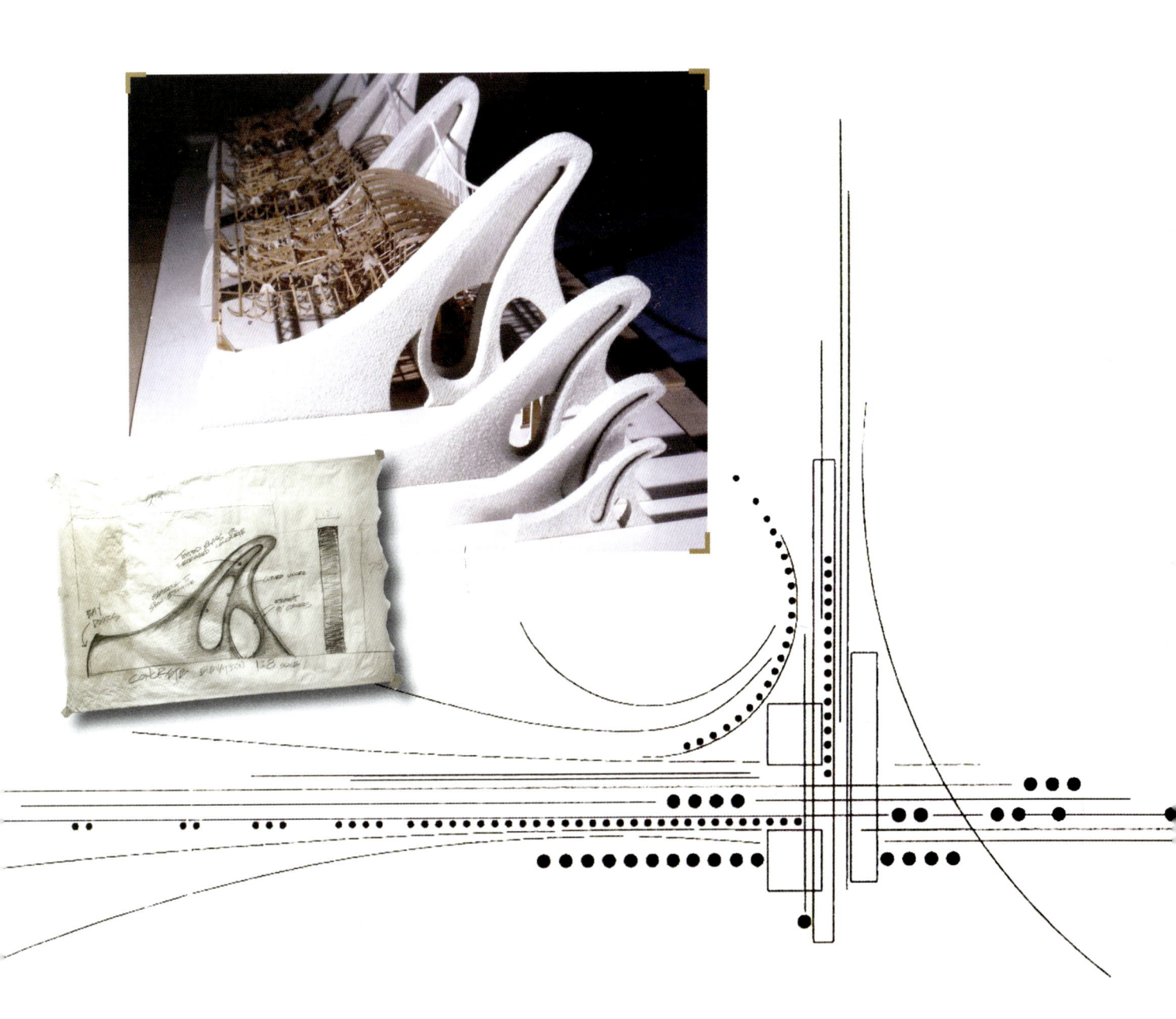

|COLLEGE YEARS

himself in as many artistic disciplines as possible whilst searching for his niche. His can-do attitude and sheer determination to create meant that he involved himself in learning an array of art forms: fine art, design, commercial design, graphic design, ceramics, carpentry, industrial arts, drafting, plastics and finally architecture. Though his commitment to creativity meant getting his hands dirty and committing to learning different disciplines, the time eventually came when he started to understand that in order to better apply himself to his art it was imperative that he began to take an analytical approach to his studies. With a sudden interest in academic focus, Adam began to scour through textbooks to learn geometry, algebra, color theory and application, and his vision of art and creativity began to take on a far more mature and three-dimensional state. Despite a heavy engagement into different artistic disciplines, the hours spent analyzing and building with LEGO bricks still resonated within him. The involvement of model making made architecture a thoroughly attractive vocation. As Adam recalls to us, the choice of what to pursue quickly became a clear and logical decision.

"I came to realize that I didn't like studying art. Art wasn't structured enough for me, it wasn't disciplined enough. I felt like it was too ambiguous and you could do anything you wanted to do. Once I applied myself I became good at math and geometry, and when I looked at the practical and theoretical application of art and science, and in my opinion, the result is architecture."

With a firm grasp on what he wanted to do after high school, Adam started to apply for colleges. Despite being a self-confessed 'bad student', he had a thorough and extensive high school portfolio that he could use to engage potential colleges. After being accepted into three colleges, Adam decided to accept an offer from Kansas State University – an unlikely choice given that it was not only a considerable distance from Adam's home of Chicago but it was also in a rather isolated location. In September 1991, Adam made the move from Chicago to Kansas to begin his five-year training as an architect.

Despite his doubts, once Adam began the program he realized Kansas was the right place for him as the program focused heavily on the art and design side of architecture rather than textbook study. Their theory was that zoning codes and concrete mixtures were lessons that had to be learnt, but by using the first few years to craft and explore your own style as a designer, you could graduate with a more focused and stylized portfolio, and ultimately be more employable at the end of the course. For Adam, this allowed him to mould his style as well as his own identity as an architect, which is something other schools may have not allowed him to achieve. Adam's style emphasized structure; Adam focused his studies on organic design, philosophy and design theory, building upon his knowledge of shape and color relationships whilst gaining a deeper insight into creating spaces and placement approach. With budgets, gravity wind loads, seismic conditions and other learnable material left to

Kansas State University campus where Adam studied Architecture.

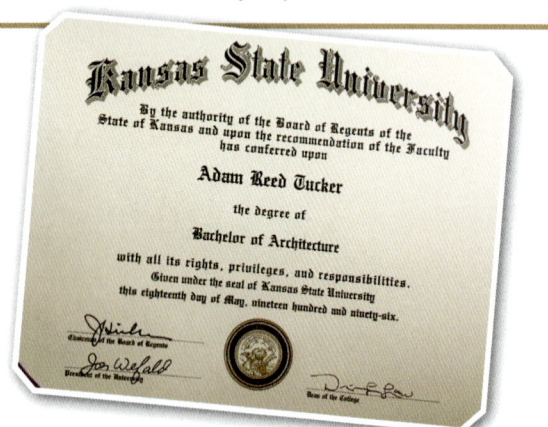

"I came to realize that I didn't like studying art. Art wasn't structured enough for me, it wasn't disciplined enough. I felt like it was too ambiguous"

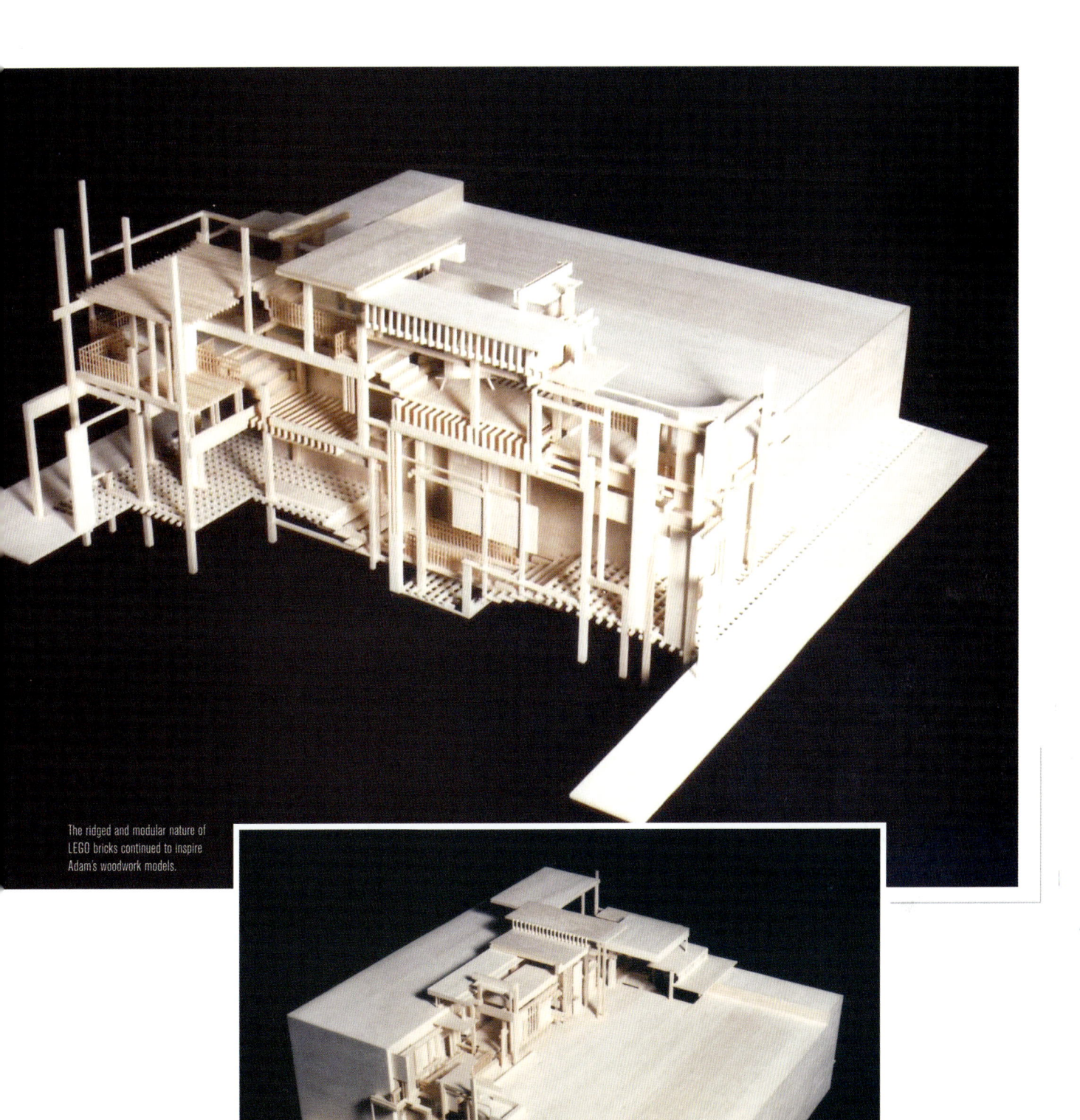

The ridged and modular nature of LEGO bricks continued to inspire Adam's woodwork models.

BRICKSCULTURE 17

|COLLEGE YEARS

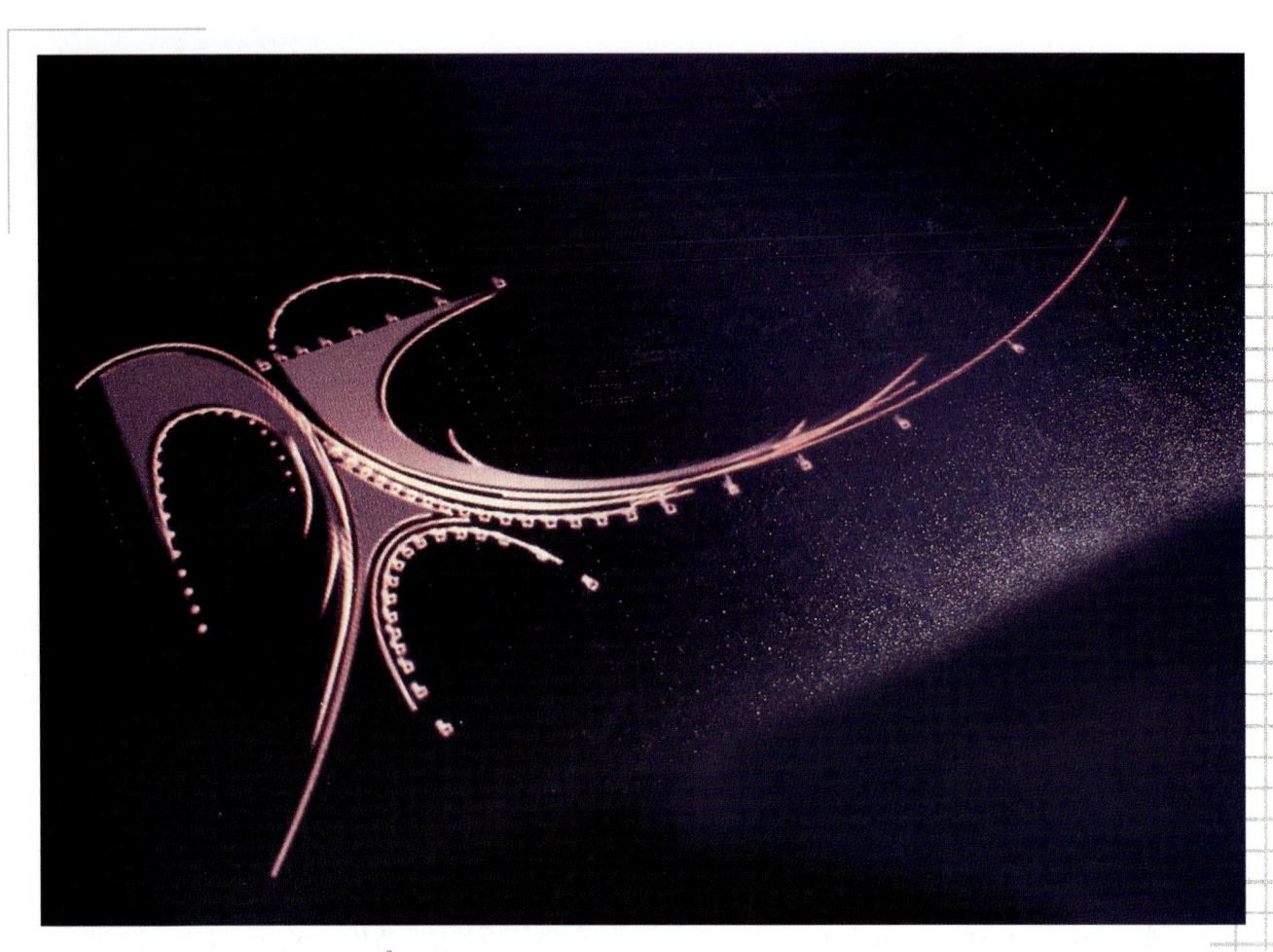

the last three years, Adam spent his first couple of years at college further exploring artistic forms and his potential style of design, eventually leading to an interest and appreciation for religious architecture.

"I enjoyed religious architecture thoroughly because it is what's known as set piece architecture, meaning they are sculptural," explains Adam. The emphasis on sculpture and sculptural theory means that set piece architecture is not designed within the restrictions of the neighboring style in which it resides. Also, as it is a stand-alone project, there's much more freedom to create something that breaks the architectural norm based on the available space. In religious architecture, the form follows the function of the space and the function of the space follows the form, as Adam explains: "I was drawn to it because the outside is usually a reflection of the inside spacing, which is created to evoke a certain emotion in a person. That to me is interesting because through emotion it becomes attached to humanity." The study of religious architecture really pushed Adam to combine all of his skills in design theory, architecture and philosophy to create spaces that affected the viewers and inhabitants. With the freedom of interaction Adam could subtly manipulate the space to create varied dynamics out of a static object.

Whilst it may seem like model making and LEGO bricks go hand in hand, it didn't initially cross Adam's mind that he may be able to bring his bricks out of retirement and use them for his studies. At this point, Adam mainly used basswood, a relatively expensive material preferred amongst students for its finer detail and cleaner look. This didn't hinder his creativity, as he happily explored any mediums from museum board and construction paper to balsa wood, straws and toothpicks, essentially using anything to achieve the projects goals. LEGO bricks must have been a bit of a campus rarity, but luckily for modern architect students, a few years later Adam would make sure he changed that.

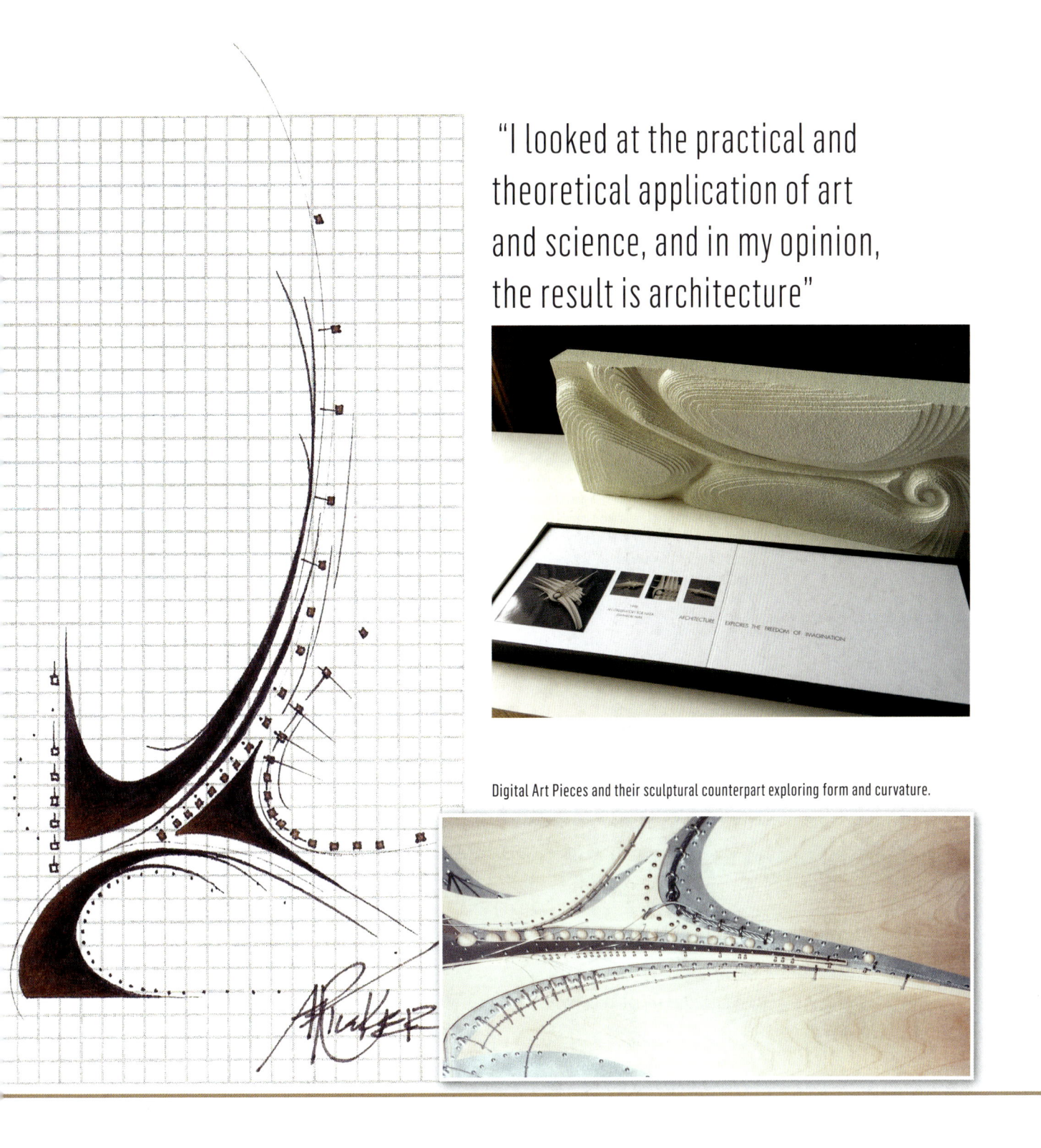

"I looked at the practical and theoretical application of art and science, and in my opinion, the result is architecture"

Digital Art Pieces and their sculptural counterpart exploring form and curvature.

COLLEGE YEARS

Adam proved to be more adept to college study than he was in high school and, during his final year, he applied for two internships. Deciding that he would never settle for second best, Adam applied for the two companies that he had a strong emotional attachment to: Lucasfilm – a division in LucasArts – and Disney. The Disney Imagineers dream died on the vine rather quickly as at the time they were only accepting applications for fine-arts interns, however after being faced with uncertainty and a nervous wait LucasArts accepted Adam as an architecture intern. It may come as a bit of a surprise that Adam should find himself working as an architect in a film production company, however Adam was hired based on the strength of his portfolio which showed a significant prowess and passion for, you guessed it, model making. The foundations of his LEGO lifestyle began to support and shape his career. Adam's role within the company would be to work on scenes for LucasArts that would appeal to his model-making finesse,

"I am horrible at illustrating, to this day I really can't sketch well, but I was good at putting models together and set design was something that they saw within my portfolio." Hooked on the appeal of this amazing opportunity, Adam quickly sorted the paperwork to hand into his university, however a stumbling block stifled his excitement and quickly brought the opportunity to a grinding halt.

Kansas State University had strict rules over internship course credits and, unfortunately for Adam, working as a set designer for LucasArts was far too close to drama school and was simply outside architecture's periphery to justify a course credit. The internship still stood for Adam, but it was unpaid and Adam would have to justify taking an extra year in college, as well as trying to fund the six months away from home. After seeking counsel from his father and weighing up the pros and cons of the situation, Adam decided that despite it looking good on his resume the extra year at University would hinder Adam's progress in the long run and the

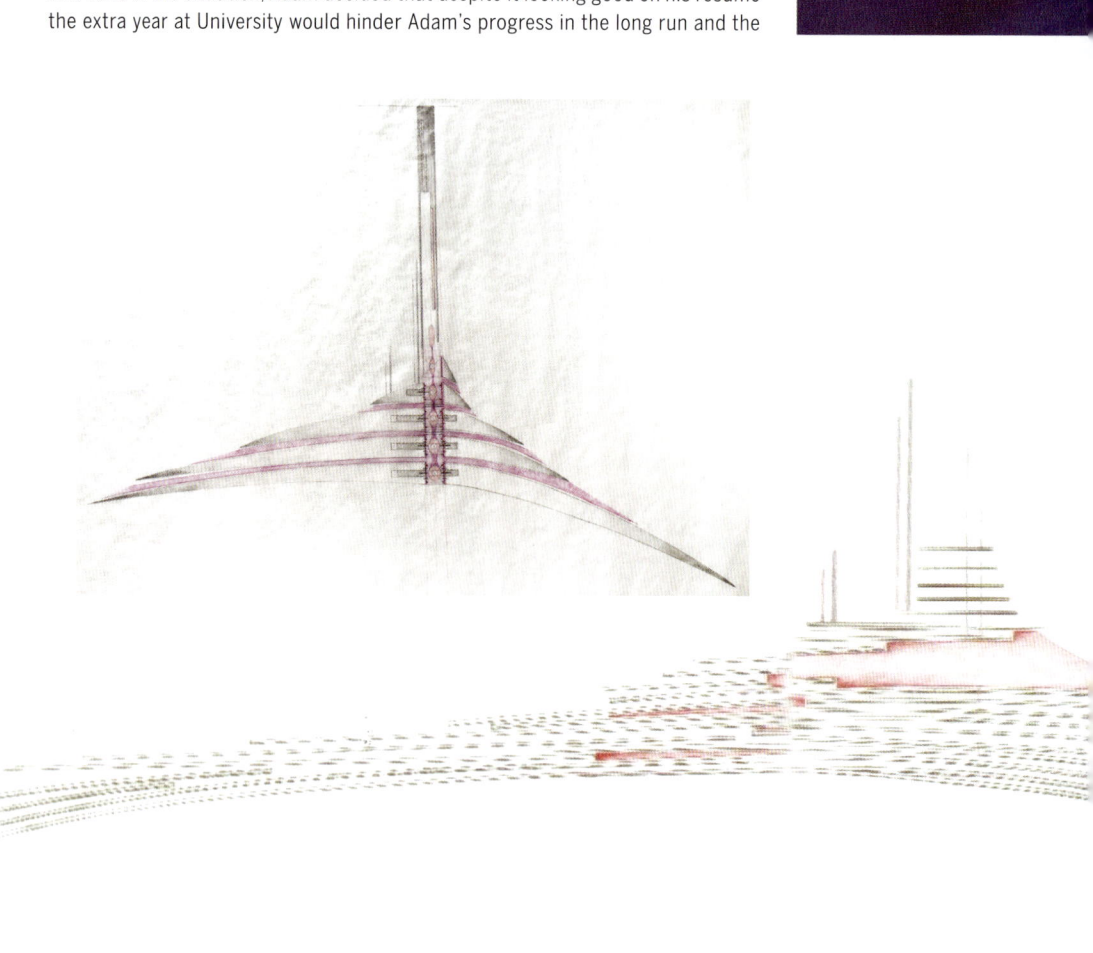

Adam's senior thesis project at KSU.

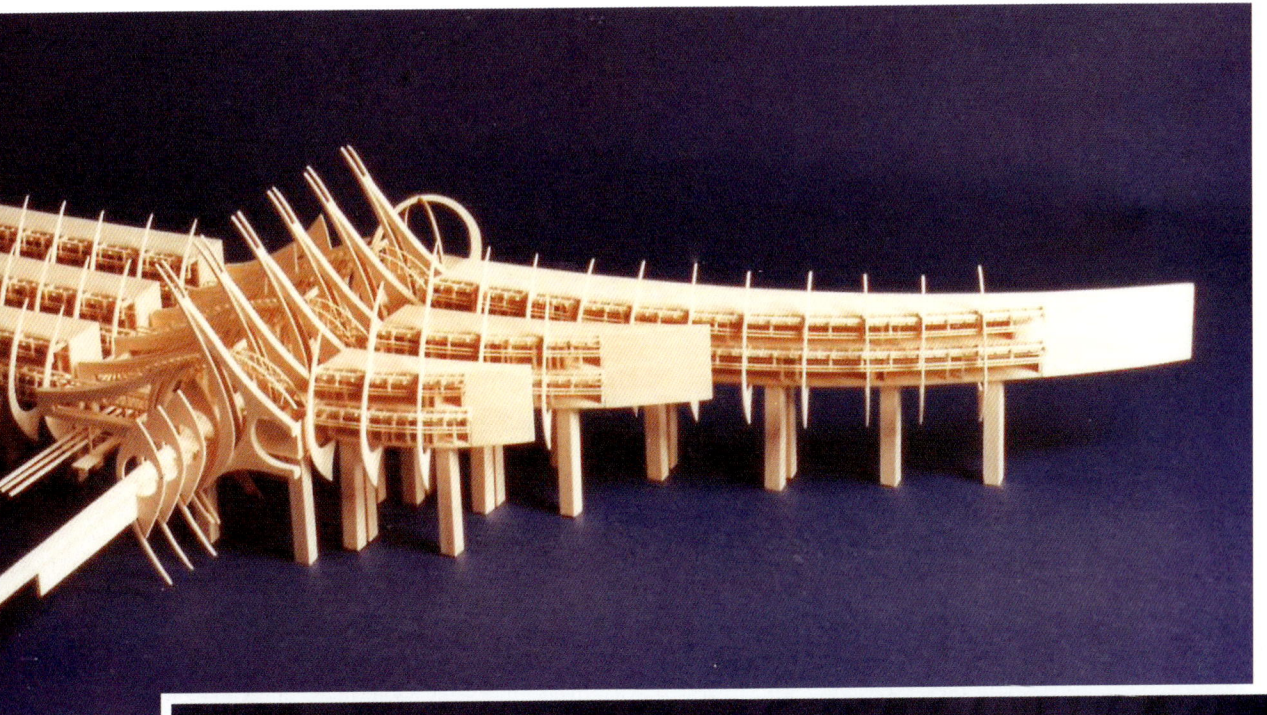

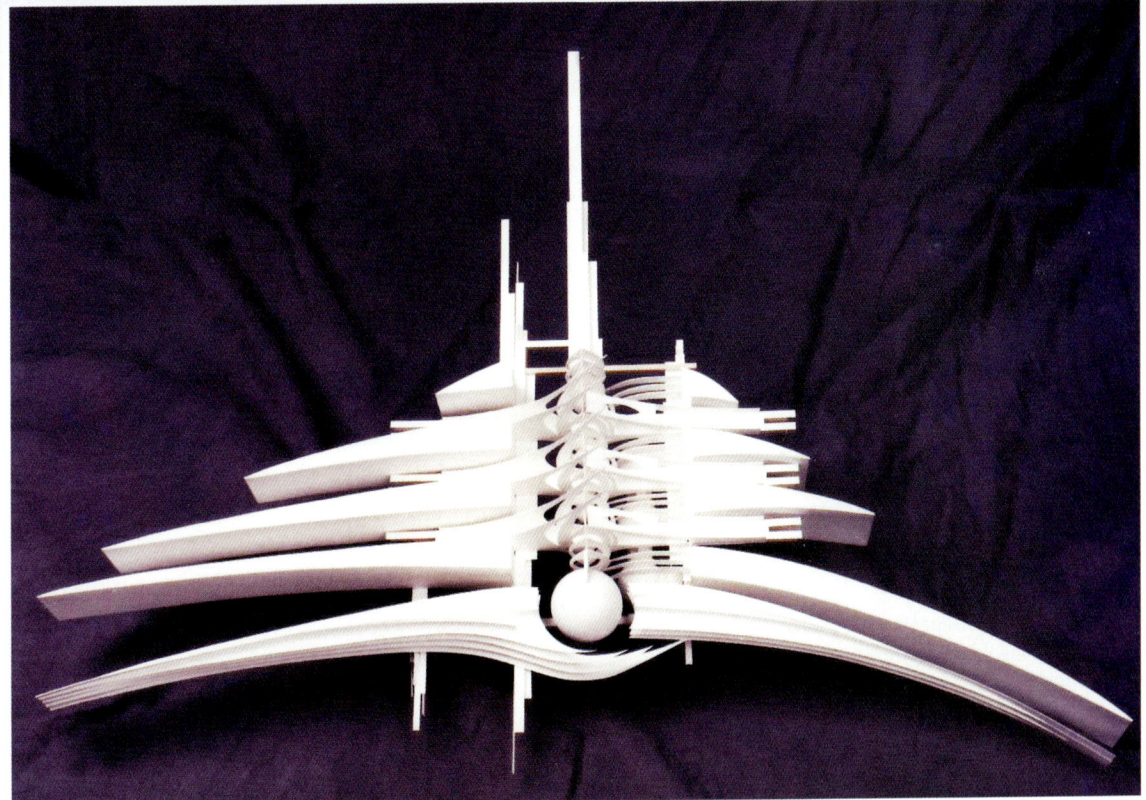

|THE COLLEGE YEARS

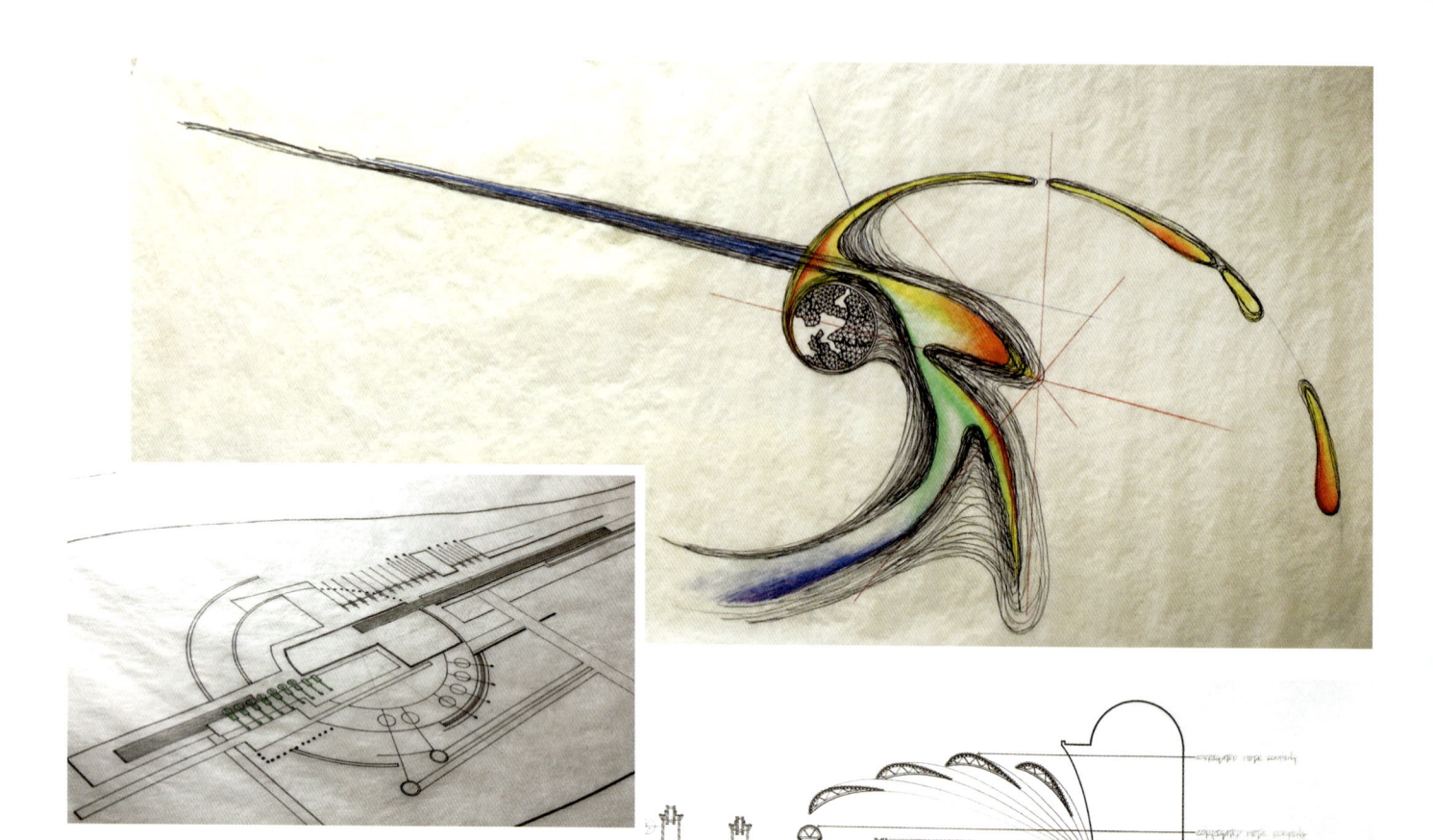

internship was never realized.

There was another option for Adam. Rather than taking on an internship there was the choice to take a course called Independent Studies, which consisted of creating a thesis and researching it before applying it to a real-world scenario. Building on his previous work in transitions, form and morphing, Adam decided to do a study on how shapes morph within a space. The overall theme of his thesis was 'Philosophy of Design Theory' with particular focus on behaviorism and aesthetics in organic architectural design. Although it proved to be a wise move to continue to study and apply design theory, Adam found he sorely missed the opportunity to take on the LucasArts internship, especially once he discovered that he would have been making set models for Star Wars Episode One: The Phantom Menace.

Although it may be disappointing to know that you could have spent six months working on a fascinating project, and adding to the rich canon of a world you know and love, all was not lost. After all, why spend six months creating models for one brand you love, when you can spend a lifetime creating, expanding and influencing another? When it came to getting a foot into The LEGO Group, Adam would not be so hesitant.

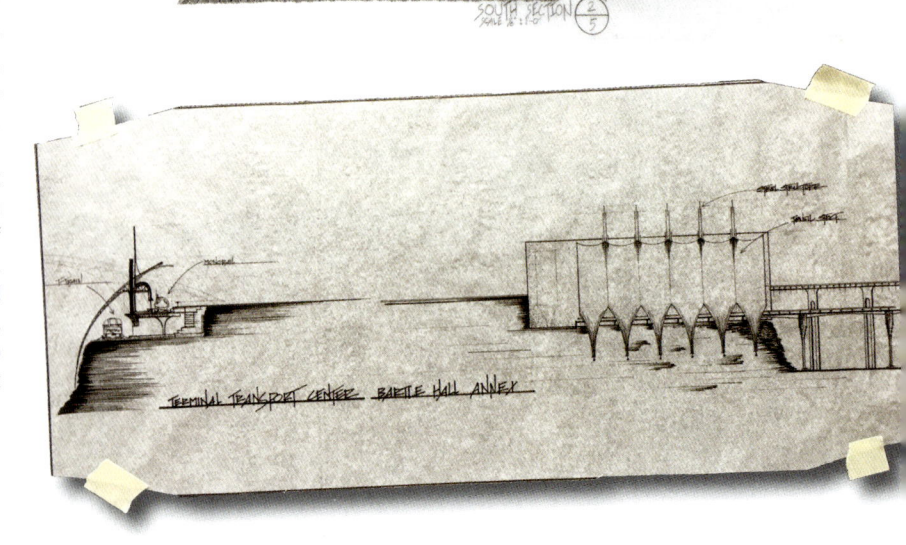

BRICKSCULTURE 23

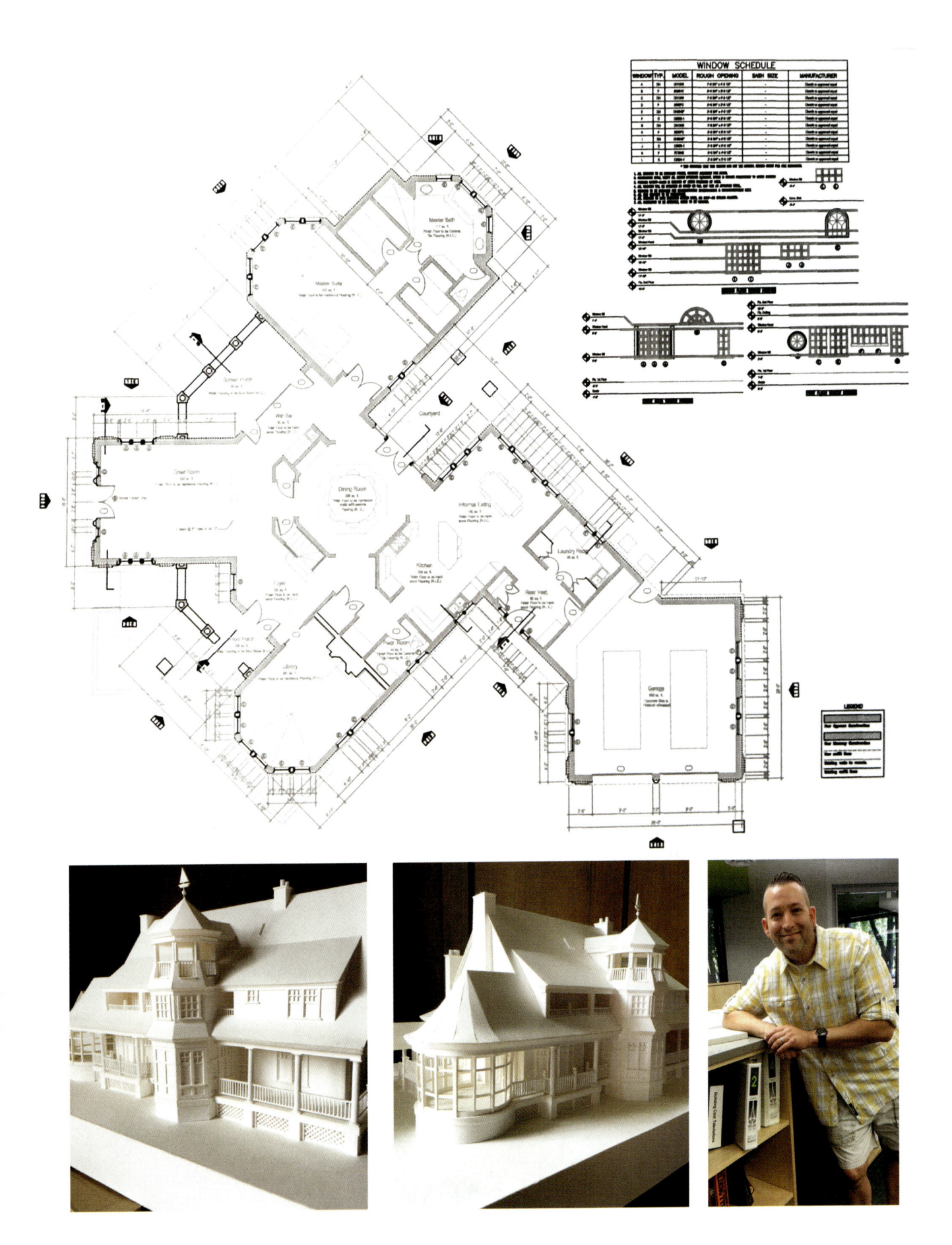

|COLLEGE YEARS

LIGHT AT THE END

How the introduction of the Star Wars LEGO theme brought Adam, and many other fans, back to the brick

Like many children in the 1970s, Adam had a strong affiliation with the Star Wars franchise. From first seeing the film as a child in 1977, to buying the action figures and building a Girders and Panels Death Star play set, it was as much a part of his childhood as LEGO bricks. Naturally the notion of not being able to take up the LucasArts internship was frustrating, however Star Wars Episode One: The Phantom Menace would ultimately put LEGO sets back in Adam's hands. Whilst searching for architectural supplies in hobby shops, Adam happened to stumble across one of the first Star Wars LEGO sets. Filled with nostalgia, and gripped with excitement, the impulse to indulge proved too much and Adam bought a few to take home and see what they were like.

"I never collected them, I never played with them, I don't even know if I built any of them. I got caught up in the moment because I was a Star Wars fan." It's a very familiar story to many adult fans of LEGO (AFOL) who were brought back to the brick in the early 2000s.

The release of Star Wars LEGO sets gripped the attention of many Star Wars fans due to the high desirability of Star Wars merchandise, a theme that goes back to the 1977 release of Star Wars Episode IV: A New Hope and the first wave of action figures. It comes at no surprise that many fans who have, or did, collect Star Wars merchandise would be so easily swept into the impulse of picking up a couple of Star Wars LEGO sets. While Adam bought the sets but neglected to open them or start collecting the series, there were many soon-to-be AFOLs who bought these

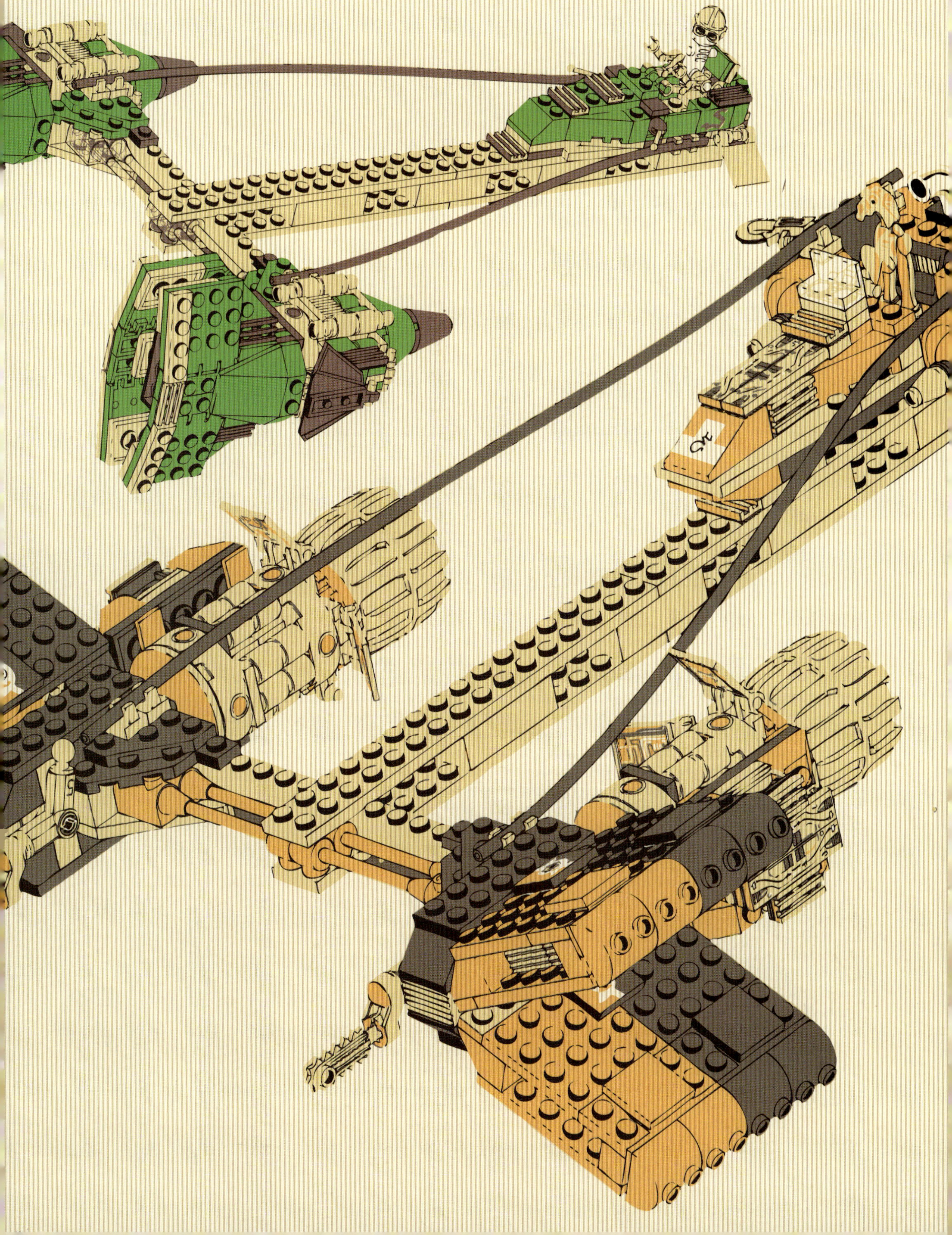

|COLLEGE YEARS

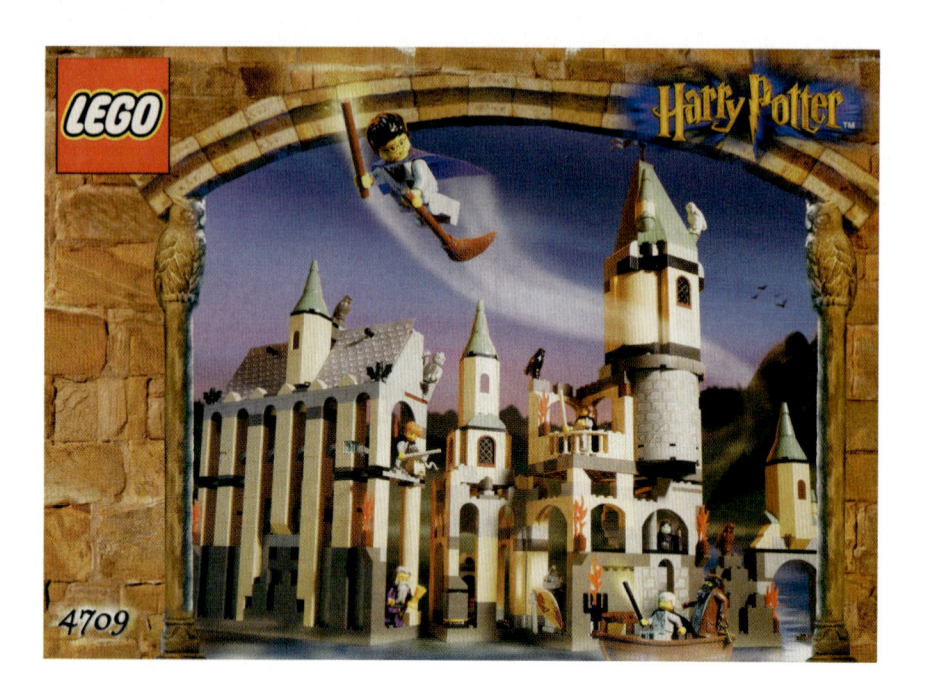

"I don't even know if I built any of them. I got caught up in the moment because I was a Star Wars fan"

sets and with it bought into the LEGO brand as a whole. Star Wars just happened to be a well-placed catalyst. The power behind the Star Wars brand is not only in its narrative, its structure, artwork, characters and environments, but in the way that it deals so well with themes that are universally relatable to all ages. It isn't a standard space or sci-fi film. The likes of R2D2 and C3PO are as much children entertainers as they are narrative devices and there is a humor and level of humanity within the films that cries out to the adult viewers. They truly are family movies you will enjoy as much when you first see it as when you watch it thirty years later. It's that emotional connection we all share which makes us reach for almost anything with a Star Wars logo on the box. This was certainly the case for Adam when in 1999 he reached for those Star Wars LEGO sets. A new generation of adults rediscovered those fantastic little bricks as a great way to spend not only quality time with the family, or connecting with their children, but also a way to escape from the stresses of everyday life. The boxes were opened and away we built.

The LEGO Group, and indeed the public's attitude towards the brick, began to change a lot in between Adam packing his LEGO bricks in the garage as a child and buying his first Star Wars set. For a lot of people building models with LEGO bricks was still a hobby surrounded in secrecy because of the stigma that it was only a kids toy. However when brave builders started to use the brick as a medium for serious model making, and use the Internet as a tool to find other fans that were doing the same, there was the sudden realization between the tech-minded AFOLs that they were not as alone as they once thought. With the advent of the Internet, and social media's rapid expansion in 2006, AFOLs began to communicate and share their passion and ideas more than they ever did before. Suddenly, a worldwide community had formed which quickly began to expand and is still expanding today. It may be human nature to want to hide something that feels like it's against the status quo, but there is strength in numbers, and as people supported their fellow builders and shared ideas amongst themselves, the hobby grew stronger and the journey of the brick evolved.

Although Adam may have purchased those Star Wars sets and hidden them away without telling anyone, by 2006 he would soon meet, become influenced and ultimately produce content for the worldwide family of AFOLs.

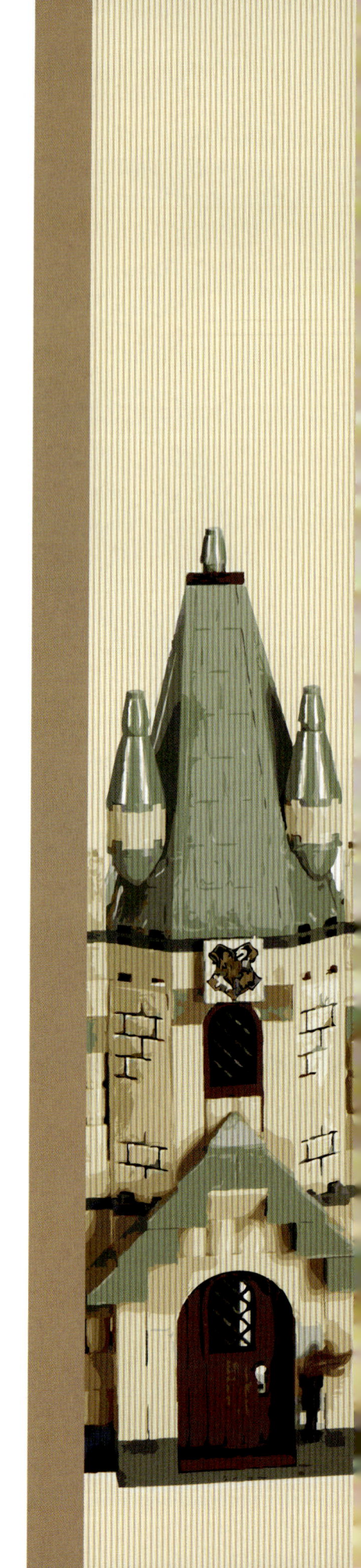

"It's that emotional connection we all share which makes us reach for almost anything with a Star Wars logo."

| THE PROFESSIONAL YEARS

THE
PROFESSIONAL
YEARS

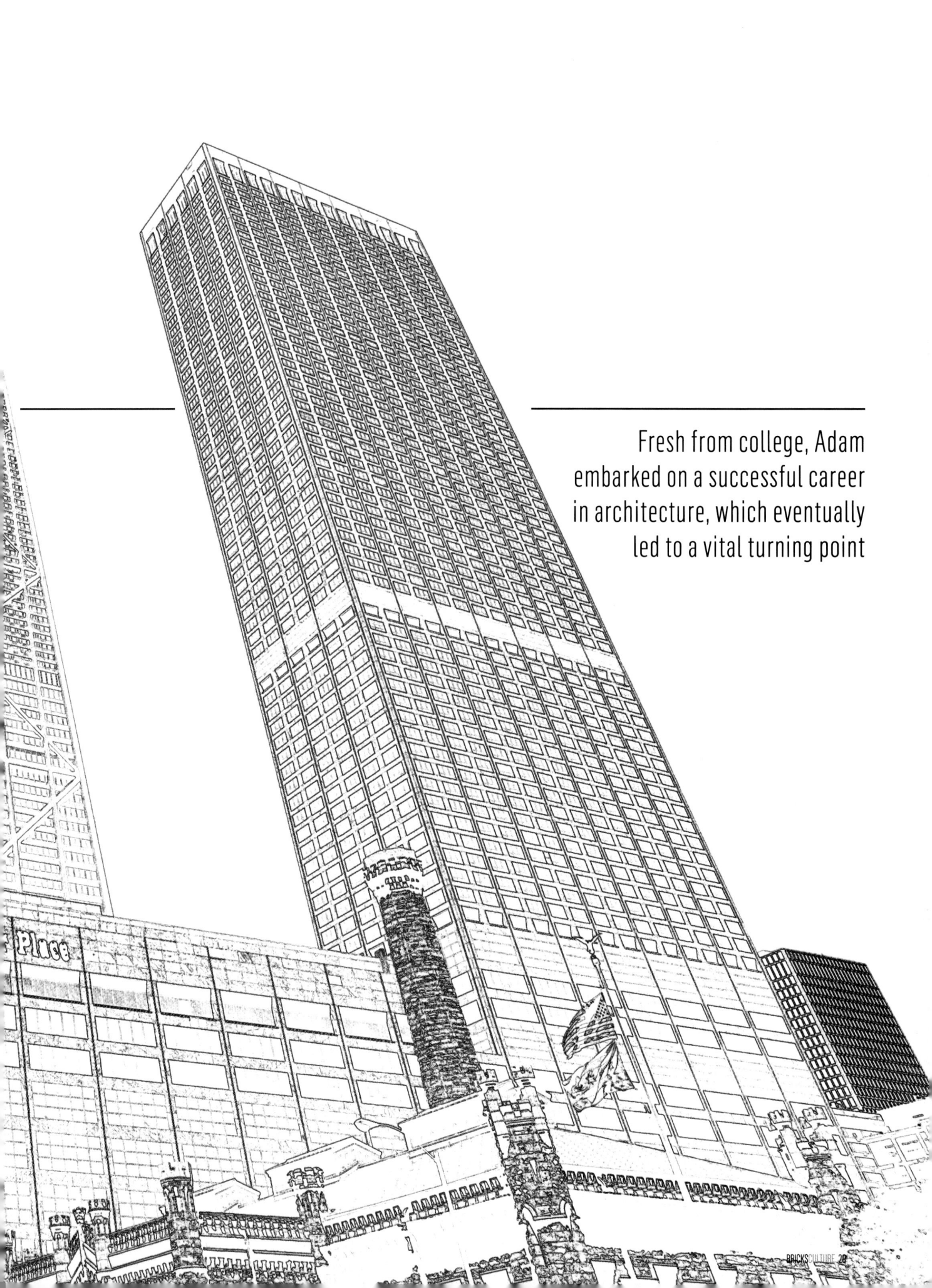

Fresh from college, Adam embarked on a successful career in architecture, which eventually led to a vital turning point

| THE PROFESSIONAL YEARS

With a LEGO collection consisting of a few Star Wars sets, Adam remained unaware of the LEGO community that had sprung up in his absence. It would be a few years before he realized his potential with the medium, and far longer before he engaged with The LEGO Group on a personal level.

Stepping back a few years to 1996, fresh from Kansas State University with a Professional Bachelor Degree in Architecture, Adam knew exactly what direction he wanted to take. "I wanted to work for the biggest and best firm in the world and at that time it was SOM, Skidmore Owings & Merrill. SOM were certainly giants in the architecture business and boast a portfolio consisting of the Sears Tower, John Hancock Centre and the largest building in the world at the time of publication: the Burj Khalifa. They have a formidable reputation amongst architects and as their portfolio suggests they specialize in building fifty-story-plus skyscrapers, which suited Adam's high ambitions perfectly. Skyscrapers are built following the same ideals that religious architecture complies with, so as stand-alone buildings their style is not dictated by its context. Rather, a successful skyscraper will begin to dictate and influence the style of the skyline. Their permanent nature requires them to be as much a monumental piece of art as a functioning building. Having high expectations as a fresh graduate must have proven a hit with SOM as, even though it was the first job he applied for, they accepted his application as a full-time architect. Unfortunately for SOM, by the time they accepted his application Adam had other ideas in mind.

"I wanted to work for the biggest and best firm in the world"

A view of the John Hancock Centre as viewed from ground level.

THE PROFESSIONAL YEARS

SOM would have provided Adam with a great resume and a continuous and consistent 30-year career, but it already employed a huge host of architects and the fight to stand out was ruthless. The journey would have been long, and Adam would spend an untold amount of time in his career following rather than leading. The progression path at SOM also started with a minimum of two years doing subsidiary design work, like bathroom tile layouts, rather than building upon his knowledge and creating his own structures. In desperate need of a position that would allow him to learn with hands-on experience at a quick pace, Adam took a job at a small firm, in a small town, on a small wage, but with a big difference. At HTK, Adam would be creating structural foundations and electrical plans for the first six months and by the end of the year would find himself as project manager, a plan that would have taken 15 years to do at SOM. By being thrown in at the deep end he would instantly be able to build upon his skills and develop knowledge on how to run a small company, which would then enable him to start his own. The entrepreneurial possibilities of working at HTK suited Adam's ambition perfectly.

Determined to be in control of his own destiny, Adam spent the next ten years working as a project manager in small firms, as well as becoming the junior partner in a small firm that made high-end million-dollar homes. To work with high budgets

"The journey would have been long, and Adam would spend an untold amount of time in his career following rather than leading"

meant that Adam could express more of his artistic creativity in his builds and continue to learn with every new project. HTK had two offices; Adam spent the first three years of his career living in Kansas City, before moving to other Chicago-area firms from 2003 to 2006. By 2006, the economy in the United States was collapsing. The housing market dried up, real estate fell and contracts became harder and harder to come by. Designers and architects all began to lose work and it wasn't long before Adam and his partners split ways. Stuck with the choice of either stepping back ten years or heading into the unknown, Adam asked the vital question which perfectly encapsulates the very essence of the human condition. What do I want to do with the rest of my life?...

The Sears Tower was the source of the first Brickstructures and LEGO Architecture set.

THE LIGHT BULB MOMENT

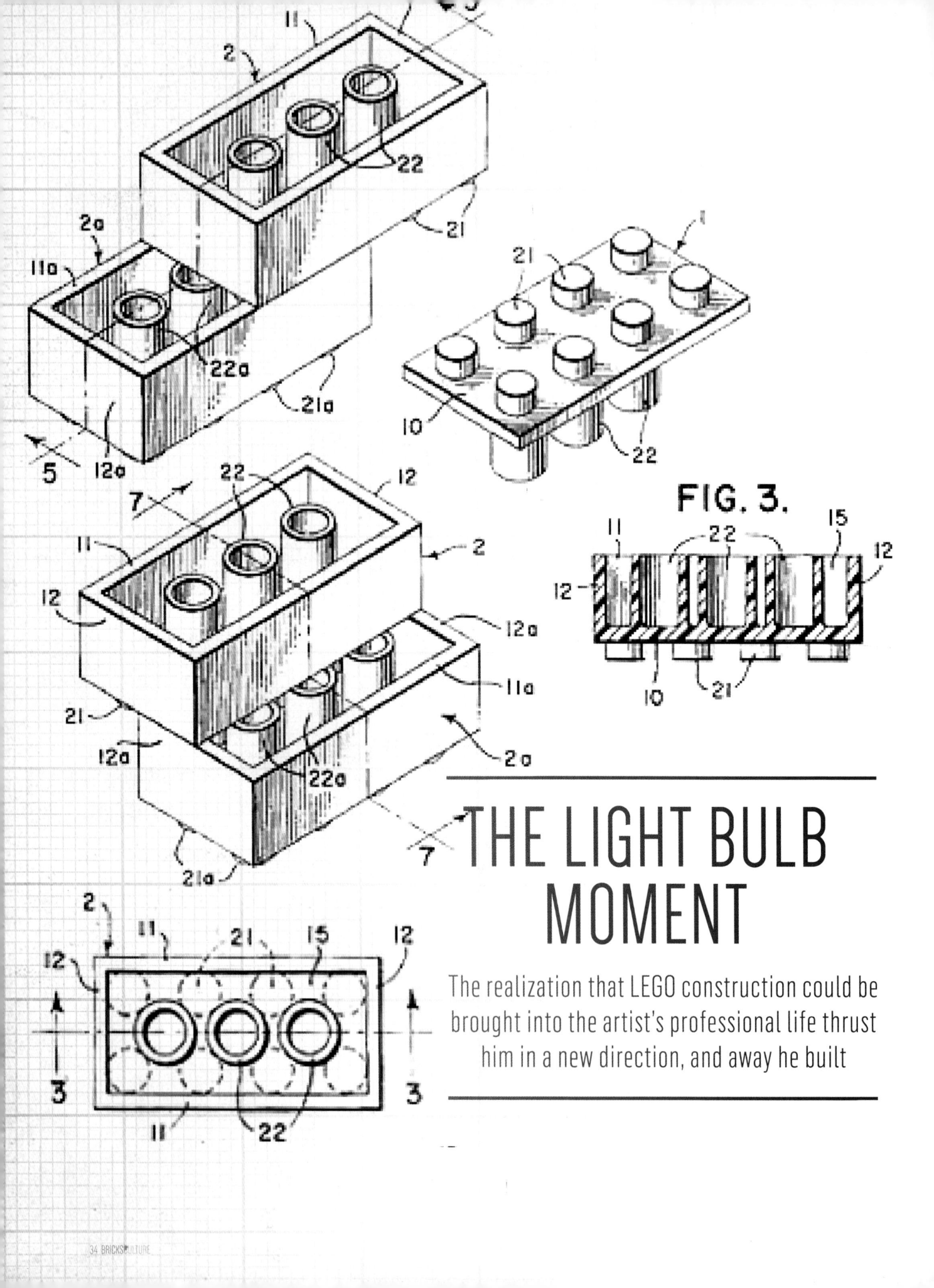

The realization that LEGO construction could be brought into the artist's professional life thrust him in a new direction, and away he built

FIG. 3.

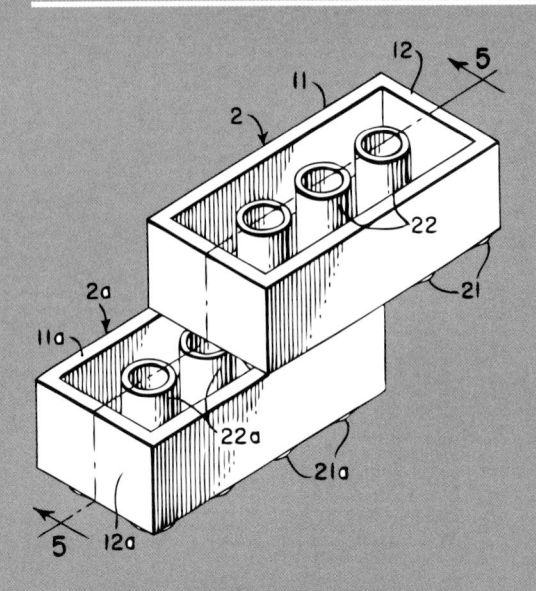

f you do what you love then you'll never work a day in your life. Although that philosophy may not be strictly true, when you find yourself at a junction in life and have time to pursue something new, asking yourself 'what do I love doing?' can often create opportunities which have laid dormant. It may be something obvious that you simply don't realize was an opportunity until that particular point in time. In Adam's case, the position he found himself in struck the very centre of his creative core. After years spent drawing and designing in architecture studios, Adam had an urge to go back to basics and use his hands to create impressive and artistic models. The urge rang true as all through his life model making had carried him and showcased not only his theoretical talents and his ability to apply them, but also his ability to create even the smallest of details with subtle flair and passion. In an age where more and more design became computer aided it seemed to be a step back into the pure and humble nature of the creator. All Adam would need is a medium. A flexible medium that required no cutting or gluing. A medium that was void of painting, and that allowed you to make and rectify mistakes without having to destroy the model. A medium that allowed for total exploration and maximum interpretation.

That's when, like two simple bricks, it clicked. "It dawned on me that LEGO bricks have the right DNA of male

> "LEGO is the equalizer. It's a simple but effective tool to express your creativity"

and female connections, they don't require great strength or specialist equipment, and if you make a mistake you can just unsnap it," reflects Adam. At that point LEGO wasn't a material that was commonly used in architecture, or even a material that was considered an asset in architectural design. Adam knew that if his idea was going to work he would have to start with a simplistic minimalist approach and use basic elements to create world-famous structures. If successful it would allow him to inspire people to be creative, whilst also showing that simple bricks that many fans would have at home could give them the craftsmanship and quality they need to unleash their creativity. "LEGO is the equalizer," adds Adam. "It's a simple but effective tool to express your creativity."

With a medium in mind, it wasn't long before Adam had drawn up plans of how to make enough money to get by each year. With an estimation that he could make five models a year at a price tag of $10,000 each, Adam began to design and build with a ferocious pace and passion, starting with the Sears Tower. Aware that he didn't want the model to be perceived as a toy, Adam decided to stick to a minimalist style and focus on the building rather than surrounding trees, cars and perceived playable features. It proved to be the perfect model to begin his venture with as the tower lent itself nicely to the black square bricks, and the actual Sears Tower company could afford the $10,000 price tag. With a limited amount of people who were creating corporate scale models – let alone bespoke corporate brick-built models – Adam's work showed unique creativity, and promising business potential, which Adam was keen to explore. The key was in the artistic interpretation and for the company to see value in the Sears Tower model, as opposed to viewing it as a LEGO toy.

It was Adam's view that his unique interpretation of the subject matter, crafted by his unusual style, experience and medium would create a model whose features, scale, texture, proportions and stylistic quality would make it a true one-of-a-kind model. It was to be a subtle blend between sculptural architecture and architectural art.

BRICKSCULTURE 37

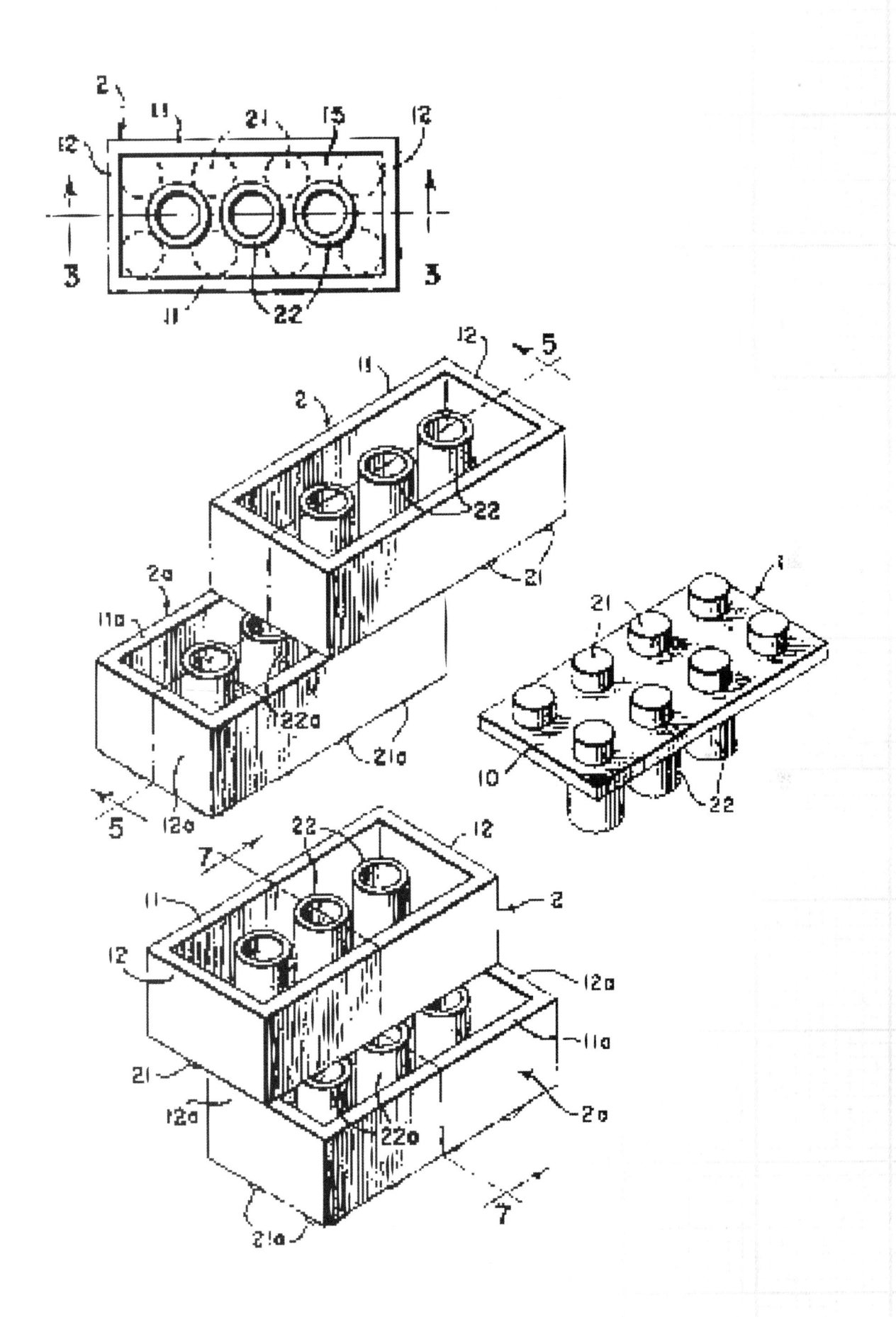

| THE HOUSE OF BRICKS

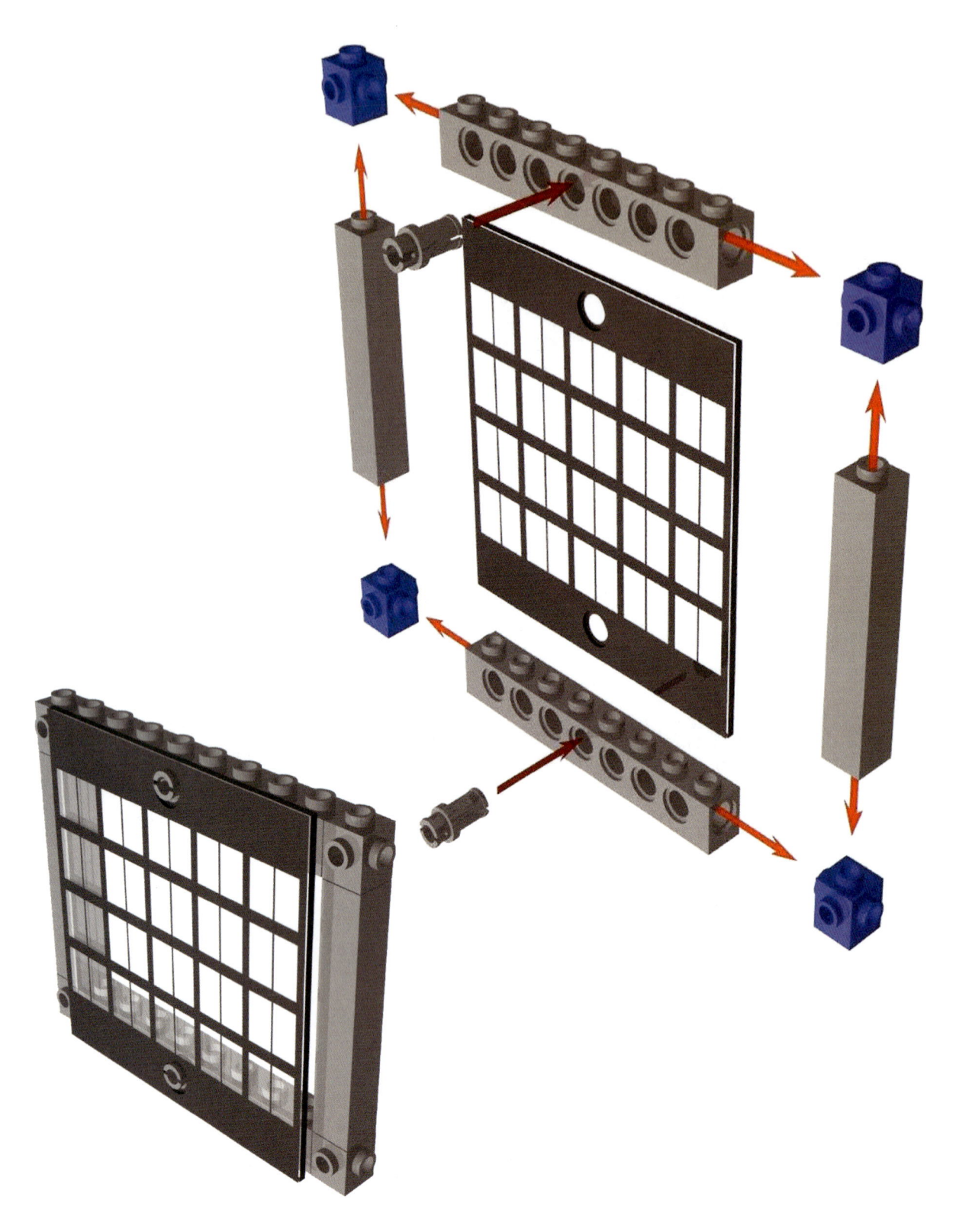

Adam's new technic pins were used to combine the play experience of LEGO with Girders and Panels.

HOUSE OF BRICKS

Equipped with an idea and a drill, Adam took matters in to his own hands to create a new kind of brick and a new artistic venture

Even though Adam's Sears Tower model was sold for the full price tag, he came to realize that the artistic world is a fickle and uncompromising beast and it would take more than a single sell to make a sustainable reputation and income. Whilst still planning, building and attempting to sell his larger skyscraper models, Adam took inspiration from his other favorite childhood toy – Kenner's Girders and Panels – and decided to try to recreate the magic of that system using LEGO bricks instead.

"I wanted to join them together because I liked the functionality of building with panels," reflects Adam, as he starts to reveal secrets which would divide the community entirely. In order to create a product that was as readily available and as versatile as LEGO bricks, but had the connections and functionality of Girders and Panels, Adam took to the online auction giant eBay and purchased in bulk as many of the Technic beams as he could. He then took to his garage and used a drill to create Technic pieces that could be positioned in both the x & z axis, rather than only having holes along the side of the bricks.

It may be far removed from any of the practices of the LEGO purist, however Adam was convinced that creating new bricks would reveal a new way of creating a more realistic framework for constructing buildings. After many hours of experimenting with bricks and drills, Adam finally found the connections he desired and so a small batch of

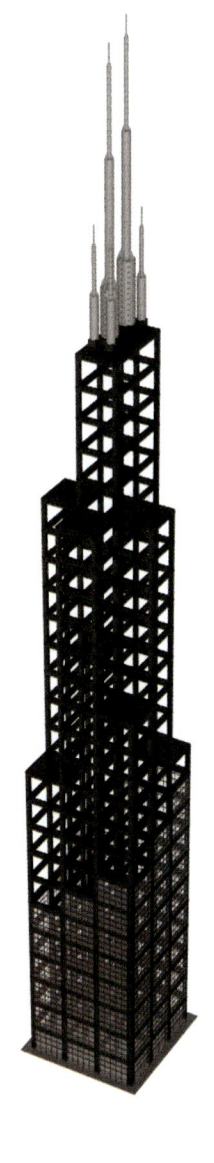

| THE HOUSE OF BRICKS

Adam holds one of the first Brickstructures sets ready to sell.

test products were created with the intention of selling them as concepts to The LEGO Group. The aim was to produce a series of kits that would make up small-scale buildings, but the more sets you bought the more you could expand your frame and ultimately the larger and more complex your frame could get. This lead to the forming of Brickstructures, Inc. and Adam had begun his venture into being a brick-entrepreneur. Once all the sets had been sorted and packaged, by hand, Adam needed a venue and an audience to sell his kits to. With the May 2006 Chicago House of Bricks quickly approaching, it seemed the perfect opportunity to give it a go and see what the fans and general public had to say about his new bricks. Signing up as an exhibitor, Adam planned to display his models including a demonstration of his new bricks, and then use that as a shop front to sell his kits on the side.

House of Bricks proved to be another turning point for Adam as, even though he turned up with the intention of gaining awareness for his work and selling his kits, he found himself engaging for the first time with the Chicago AFOL community. Everyone at the show had very different disciplines and build specialties enabling his idea and style to stand out in a very unique way. There was Felix Greco

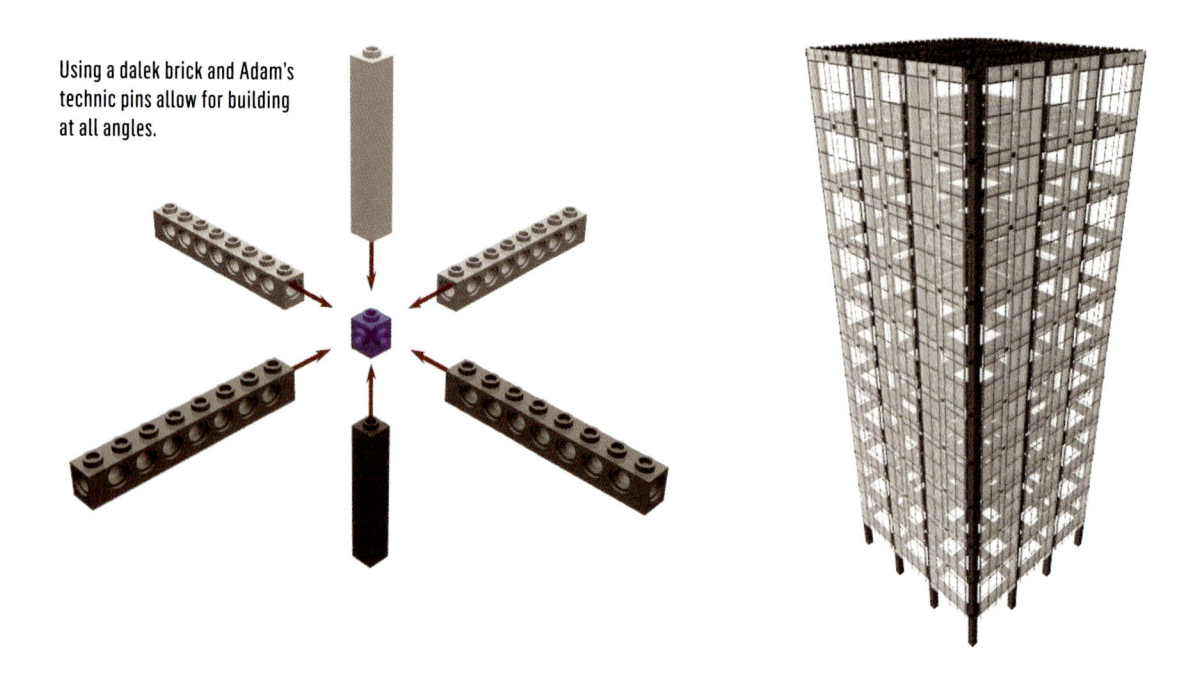

Using a dalek brick and Adam's technic pins allow for building at all angles.

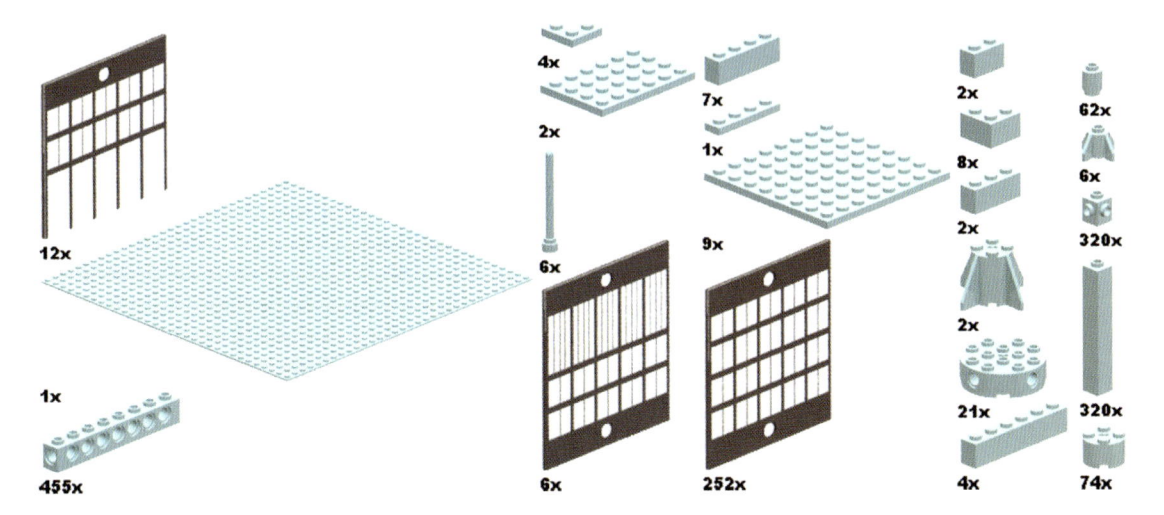

"Adam took to the online auction giant eBay and purchased in bulk as many of the Technic beams as he could, before taking to his garage and using a drill..."

Exhibitors at Brickworld crowd around Adam's skyscrapers.

THE PURIST MENTALITY

The LEGO community, like many hobbyist communities, have certain members which follow what they call 'purist' rules. The pursuit philosophy stems from the idea that official LEGO elements should only be connected to other official LEGO elements, in the correct (or 'legal') manner in which they were intended on being connected. That means no cutting, no painting, no melting, no custom printing and certainly no gluing. It's an approach that you tend to find most LEGO fans subscribe to as ultimately it promotes the sole use and purchasing of official LEGO products. Since The LEGO Group are relatively strict about their brand guidelines and the elements and colors that they produce, The LEGO Group consider any LEGO element that has been tampered in anyway to have lost its status as a LEGO brick. As a result it should technically have the LEGO branding removed from the studs. Not all fans subscribe to the purist mentality and are more than happy to buy third-party bricks, accessories and sometimes even replica LEGO sets. Whilst buying a knock-off LEGO set does nothing but harm The LEGO Group, the Bricks Culture team certainly sees no harm in using third-party products, and even LEGO-compatible products, to achieve the effect you desire with your model making.* It may not be LEGO kosher, but thinking creatively and going outside of the box can produce some spectacular results that are impossible when only using official LEGO bricks. There aren't many exploratory builders who build with such a ferocious and virtuosic talent that every one of their models is nothing short of spectacular. But builders such as James Cherry AKA Crash Cramer, Alexander Jones AKA Orion Pax and Carl Greatrix join Adam as perfect examples of those who successfully venture beyond the limitations of LEGO bricks, whilst retaining loyalty to the form.

*This does not involve purchasing sets that are created by stealing The LEGO Group's intellectual property to create imitation sets. Bricks Culture, Brickstructures and Adam Reed Tucker would advise against doing so at all costs.

| THE HOUSE OF BRICKS

BrickStructures™
A Structural and Architectural Building System

1001

This *BrickStructures*™ Set is a flexible and challenging construction set, with the added dimension of technically authentic pieces that bring exciting and real life action to whatever is built.

Innovative 6-Node Connection

Unlimited Building Possibilities: Refer to the instruction manual included inside for examples of other exciting models that can be built with this *BrickStructures*™ Set.

Inspired by and paying homage to the 2 most creative & realistic building construction systems of the 1970's: Kenner's *Girder & Panel*™ and Lego's *Expert Builder*™

Low Rise
OFFICE BUILDING #1
221 Interlocking Pieces

Copyright © 2006 BrickStructures™ by Adam R. Tucker. All rights reserved. Product code 03.15.06.1001
LEGO ® is a registered trademark of LEGO Group. *Kenner* ® is a registered trademark of Hasbro, Inc. Kenner's *Girder & Panel*™ and Lego's *Expert Builder*™ are property of their parent companies. This building set is not authorized or endorsed by either entity. Adult supervision required. Chocking Hazard – small parts.

Visit www.BrickStructures.com

Adam's technic pins have a hole drilled at the end to allow for connections at extra angles compared to normal LEGO technic beams.

"Adam was convinced that creating new bricks would reveal a new way of creating a more realistic framework for constructing buildings"

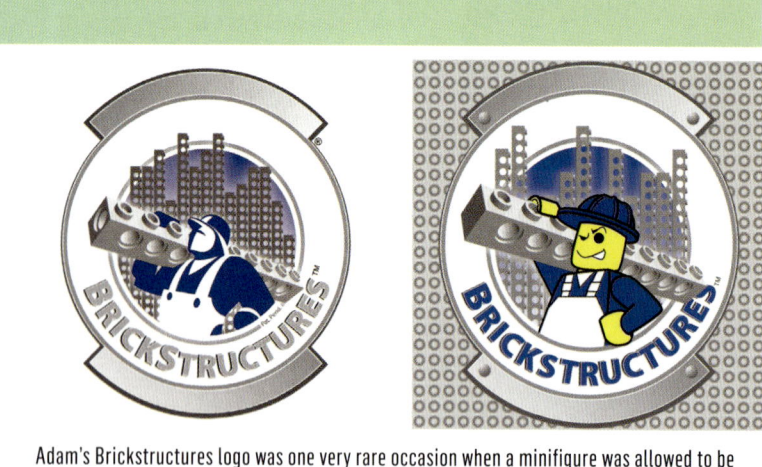

Adam's Brickstructures logo was one very rare occasion when a minifigure was allowed to be incorporated into the design.

with his custom-built characters, Mindstorms specialist Bryan Bonahoom giving demonstrations, as well as lots of exhibitors who brought their own private creations. For Adam, it was his architecture models and his custom sets that made him stand out. Everyone came from different backgrounds and yet the social playing field was leveled as all met and bonded over a common love for the brick.

Fortunately for Adam, taking a risk and going against the purist mentality by manipulating his bricks to create something new paid off. Not only did it provide him something unique to display and sell, it supplied a talking point from which he could start to interact and open a discourse with. Who was this person who came into the community with giant structures to display, and bricks that he had manipulated himself? Is he an AFOL? Is he a madman? Is he a maverick? No one could put their finger on it. This did not stop the public from taking interest in Adam's custom Brickstructures sets and, before the end of the event, Adam had sold out of his stock and put a healthy $500 in his pocket. The money he earned didn't stay in his pocket for long as Adam had other ideas and put the money straight back into Brickstructures. A brand had been created and it wouldn't be long before Brickstructures would be brought to the attention of The LEGO Group.

An example of a structure built using Adam's Brickstructures set.

GIRDERS AND PANELS

Kenner's Girders and Panels played an important part in the transition from metal toys of the 1920s to the plastic toys of the modern age. Girders and Panels is also arguably the only construction toy that accurately reflects play through modern building techniques. The building system started off with simple girders clicking into a baseboard and then interlocking within one another, then with the attachment of thin plastic panels you could create giant structures with ease. Although it started out as a relatively simple building system, like any successful toy it ended up evolving and soon you could incorporate roof panels, roadways, truss bracing, and battery motors to create more and more complicated structures. With a bit of imagination it was possible to build motorized drawbridges, elevators and even a monorail. A whole range of motorized structures could be at your fingertips with a few girders and a few panels. Kenner went on to release over 30 sets before being sold to General Mills, then Irwin Toys and finally Bridge Street Toys. There are now over 80 sets, with many becoming iconic and rare sets which command a high price on the resale market.

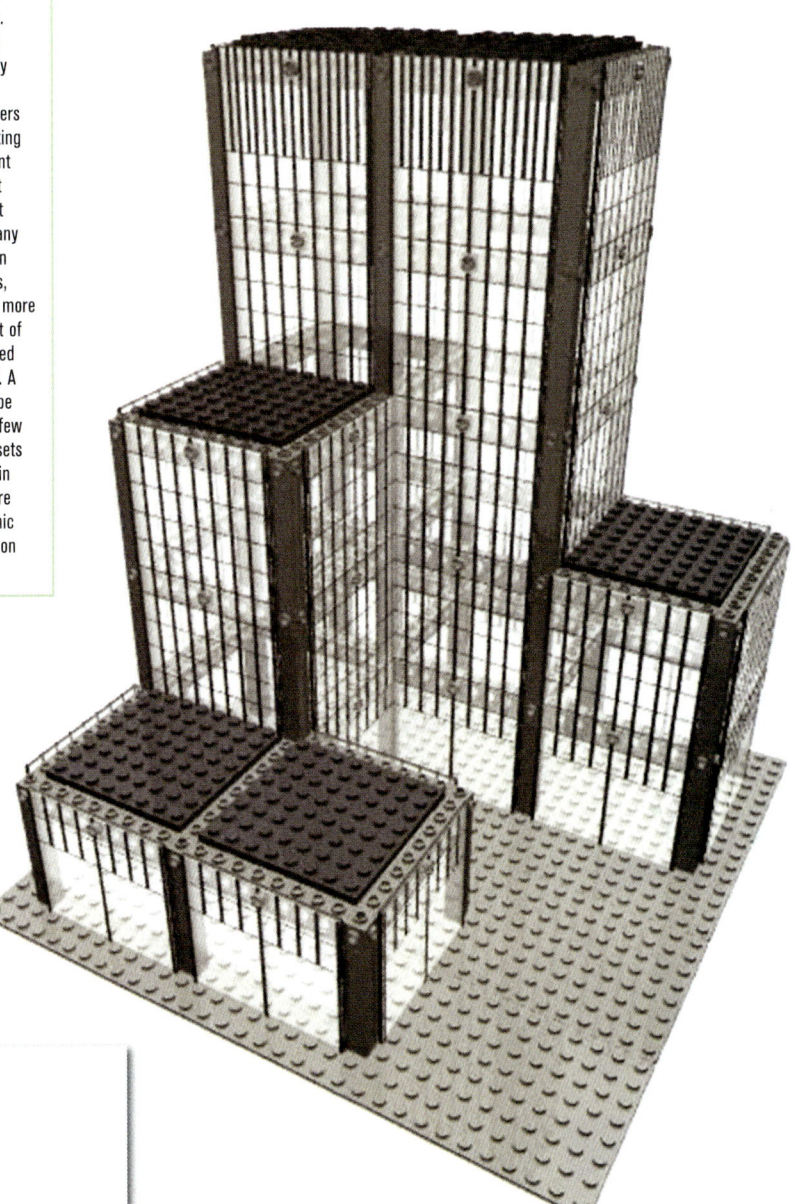

"Is he an AFOL? Is he a madman? Is he a maverick? No one could put their finger on it"

|BRICKFEST

BRICKFEST
WASHINGTON

How Adam's perseverance pays off as his inspiring products catch the eye of The LEGO Group and the rest, they say, is history

Fresh from a successful first event and with a brick-built budget under his belt, Adam got back into his home studio and began to eagerly plan his next miniature set. With his recent success at designing and building a large-scale Sears Tower model, it seemed a natural development to create it on a smaller scale. After all, Adam had already done all the research and sourced reference images, as well as having lots of parts left over from the larger build, which were the right color and shapes needed. Taking to his bricks, it wasn't long before a prototype developed into a final model and Adam could move onto creating a Brickstructures Sears Tower box with instructions. This set would have to be a cut above his last efforts as Adam had set his sights on the next big show: Brickfest in Washington D.C.

With the aid of a rented moving van, Adam strapped in his large skyscraper models and packed up his Brickstructures sets ready for the 700-mile drive – a trip that would test the nerves and patience of the budding artist. "The drive was 15 hours long in an unair-conditioned van, during a blazing hot summer. Not only that but my buildings crumbled under the stress from the long drive," recalls Adam. Yet despite the all-too familiar toils that transporting LEGO models brought, Adam made it to Brickfest and put together a presentation area that literally went above and beyond the usual show exhibition stand. In-between creating his huge LEGO sculptures, his micro Brickstructures sets and diving into new concepts, Adam had found the time to build upon his software knowledge of Autocad and teach himself Adobe Premiere, Illustrator, Photoshop, Director and 3DStudio. With his newfound skills, Adam created two animations to hook in his audience. The first was an animation showing how he carved the holes to create new Technic bricks, and the second was a step-by-step animation of how to build the Sears Tower model. These two animations joined his large-scale models and mini Sears Tower sets to form an exhibition area that promised to give visitors inspiration, as well as the tools to begin to transform that inspiration into a building.

Even though every effort was made so that visitors would buy into his Brickstructures brand, Adam had another motive for pulling out all the stops at Brickfest. "I had heard that Brickfest was going to be visited by some of the staff from The LEGO Group, and I knew that this was my chance to show them the box and my set." The effort put into creating his animations paid off as, unknown to Adam at the time, it was his animation that drew in Tormod Askildsen, Senior Director of The LEGO Group. Tormod brought it to the attention of Paal Smith-Meyer, head of the New Business Group who instantly saw the magic in Adam's budding idea, despite its somewhat controversial methods. Paal recognized that Adam's creation had the potential to benefit The LEGO Group and a discussion between the three men was quickly opened. With Paal quickly solidifying the position that creating a new Technic part with the connections that Adam had designed would prove far too expensive for a prototype, and warning that it was not in The LEGO Group's ethos to freely manipulate bricks, the three decided to test Adam's idea by creating a range of souvenir sets. With the revenue generated from the test sets, they could start to explore further kits and concepts to gauge the mileage in Adam's idea. Ultimately, these ideas would quickly develop, adapt and grow into what we now know as the LEGO Architecture range, but it would not be a smooth and easy ride for Adam. It would involve a lot of work, a lot of building and a lot of determination. But Adam was more than prepared to go above and beyond to make his ideas flourish and his art succeed.

Adam's set-up dwarfs other exhibitors, and continues to do so when finished.

Having met Bryan Bonahoom at the House of Brick event the pair became good friends. Here Bryan lends a hand, little did they know that soon they would become business partners for Brickworld.

Some of Adam's structures are so tall a crane is needed to fully assemble them.

Adam debuts his Brickstructures alongside his large collection of brick-built skyscrapers.

BRICKSCULTURE 45

THE BEGINNING OF ARCHITECTURE

Launching Brickstructures, and his landmark architecture kits, was a labour intensive process that saw Adam doing everything from packing sets, promoting them and delivering the final product to retail outlets. But it was a process that paid off...

Adam packing and overseeing the entire set production process.

Adam and Jonny Geiselman, regional buyer for Accent Chicago gift shops, with a new line of the Brickstructures set.

BRICKSCULTURE 47

|BECOMING CERTIFIED

48 BRICKS CULTURE

GETTING CERTIFIED

What is the elite LCP program and how would joining be the start of Adam building his architectural LEGO empire? Read on to find out...

With a dialogue now open between Adam and The LEGO Group, and budding business on the horizon, the company looked for ways to bring Adam into the fold. Tormod Askildsen, Senior Director of Community Engagement and Events, and Head of New Business Group Paal Smith-Meyer were convinced Adam's talents were good enough to uphold the brand's guidelines and wanted to secure the artist's ideas, ventures and resource by incorporating him into The LEGO Group. The only question was: How? Adam's place in the LEGO universe wasn't clear. He was not a fully-fledged AFOL, he was too artistic to be corporate material and he couldn't fit directly into the design team because that would involve him moving to The LEGO Company's headquarters in Billund, Denmark, which Adam wasn't prepared to do. Still, Tormod and Paal were determined to find a way.

Within The LEGO group exists a program for exceptional entrepreneurial builders called the LEGO Certified Professional Program – or LCP's for short. To come across an LCP is somewhat of a rarity as there are only a handful of carefully selected candidates graced with the title. The LCP's job varies from person to person, with some creating bespoke creations, busts of famous people, LEGO artworks and company logos. The one thing that all the LCP's have in common is that they are all exceptional builders who are recognized by the LEGO group as proficient, professional and reliable-build resources. They must act in accordance to the guidelines of The LEGO Group and their ties to The LEGO Group not only give them a formal relationship, but it also gives them access to bricks at a much lower price than retail. Although Adam didn't specifically fit into the LCP framework, it was the only way that Tormod and Paal could see Adam being attached to The LEGO Group and retaining his business ideas whilst also allowing him the freedom to operate on a self-motivated and

BECOMING CERTIFIED

Adam with Tormod Askildsen and the other LCP's.

"The real benefit in receiving the title was the formal relationship with The LEGO Group"

self-controlled way. In 2007, Tormod and Paal approached the other six LCP's to pitch Adam as a candidate for the LCP program. The others in the program believed that Adam brought something unique to the table as there was no-one else whose aim it was to use the brick as a medium to tell the story of architecture. As it wasn't an area that was being serviced, with the approval of the other six LCP's, Tormod and Paal approached Adam with the offer. He could continue to create his own sets, with access to bricks at cost and approval from the rest of the group.

Adam's LCP story is rather unusual: the majority of LCP's apply to the position or seek out The LEGO Group to convince them why they are the perfect candidate. It's no surprise that it is a very sought-after position, as who wouldn't want the honor of being a certified professional LEGO builder? It's a title that is steeped in renown and esteem within the LEGO community – Adam is only the 7th person to receive the honor. When Paal and Tormod presented Adam with the opportunity he saw the potential of being able to purchase bricks at cost, yet the real benefit in receiving the title was the formal relationship with The LEGO Group. This would enable him to embark on the creative endeavors he wished to pursue with the full force of the LEGO brand to support him, if he required it. Exploring aspects of architecture with LEGO, and telling architecture's story through the brick would be the theme that underlined all of Adam's projects and concepts, and he still remains the only LCP to do so.

The first step once you accept the role of an LCP is to read, understand and sign the LCP contract. The contract contains the rules and regulations that The LEGO Group requires you to stick to and operate by. It's no light piece of paperwork, and as well as understanding how to act in accordance to The LEGO Group's ethics it also contains a traffic light matrix to abide by. The traffic light system is a visual representation of what subject matter you can and cannot represent in LEGO Bricks. Green means an LCP can build within that subject matter, amber means The LEGO Group have to be informed of your intentions and the relevant

David Harris - 99th General Assembly, State of Illinois: House of Representatives - presents Adam with a Certificate of Recognition.

Adam Reed Tucker

LEGO Certified Professional

| BECOMING CERTIFIED

parties involved before any contracts are signed, and red is territory you are unable to enter without any exceptions. These tend to include things that directly go against The LEGO Group's guidelines such as alcohol, drugs, violence etc. After that you are given a report to fill out in which you enter the PR, marketing, engagement, events, builds and commission the you do throughout the year. That's it. There is no hand-holding or a list of assignments you can start, there is just a swift release into the world with the LCP status. For Adam, it was all the drive he needed to start building his empire brick by brick. Adam had proved he could be an active business partner, and his work coincided with The LEGO Group's tradition in a way that they had not yet engaged in. As Adam puts it: "You are basically filling a void The LEGO Group does not fill on their own, so an LCP fills the void where LEGO knows there is an opportunity but they don't have the means, know-how or interest to do it on their own. That's where we are accommodated and do it on their behalf."

With his LCP certificate in hand but no idea when the next job or paycheck would be coming from, Adam quickly began to think about the successes he had at selling his sets – most notably in Washington. But just as quickly he remembered the appalling journey and the stress of transporting his models such a long distance to exhibit. There was only one solution. Adam reached out to others in the LEGO community who shared the same experience as him and he began to execute his first idea as a LEGO certified professional.

> "An LCP fills the void where LEGO knows there is an opportunity but they don't have the means, know-how or interest to do it on their own. That's where we are accommodated and we do it on their behalf"

Adam with his 18ft model of the Burj Khalifa at the atrium of the Elgin Public Library.

| WORKING WITH THE LEGO GROUP

BUILDING A NEW RELATIONSHIP

Having to endure the stress of traveling such a perilous distance to display his wares led to Adam, and Indianapolis-based builder Bryan Bonahoom, to develop their own show just outside of Chicago called Brickworld. As it was a decision born out of the desire to have a show closer to home, it would be a project that Adam would stay involved in until his efforts were forced to be concentrated elsewhere. The development of Brickworld however, is a tale for another chapter.

Fresh from a successful meeting and conversing with Tormod and Paal, Adam would use the first year of Brickworld Chicago as a venue to sell a self-described 'pre-test prototype' of the Sears Tower. Adam went back in to his brick studio and created a further 250 sets as limited edition one-off event kits. Brickworld was launched in June 2007 and the Brickstructures sets proved themselves to be as popular in Chicago as they did in Washington and, by the end of the first day of Brickworld, Adam successfully exceeded his expectation and sold all the sets. There was certainly a demand for these architecture-themed LEGO sets, and the sales report to Paal was met with sheer delight. The next step would be to take the sets out of the LEGO fan arena and place them into a location where the consumer was less LEGO focussed.

Back in the studio, Adam worked tirelessly as a creative surge lead to a more refined Sears Tower model and also a new John Hancock Building model. Once the model designs were finalized, The LEGO Group supplied all the parts needed to create 1,250 sets for each of the models, whilst also sending Adam permission to use their logo and the tagline 'Published by The LEGO Group' on his packaging. Whether or not the recognition of The LEGO Group's logo would help sell the product remains to be seen, but the recognition that comes with LEGO agreeing to put their brand behind a product speaks volumes about the quality, ingenuity and unique thinking behind an idea. Once the bricks arrived the absolute scale of the task at hand was truly realized; almost every room, corridor and any other available space in Adam's home was filled with the bricks required to make up 2,500 sets.

Even though the idea of having a house overflowing with LEGO bricks may be a dream to some fans, using those bricks to create and assemble 2,500 sets is no easy feat. Adam had to create the model, design the packaging,

A series of chance-taking and maverick ideas lead to the creation and fulfilment of the LEGO Architecture range

LEGO Architecture

Empire State Building
New York City, New York, USA

- Booklet included with details on design and history.
- Broschüre enthaltenen Informationen auf die Gestaltung und Geschichte.
- Livret inclus avec des détails sur la conception et l'histoire.
- Folleto incluido con detalles sobre el diseño y la historia.
- Folheto incluído com detalhes sobre o projeto e história.
- Füzet tartalmazza a részletes tervezés és történelem.

192 mm / 7.5 inches
80 mm / 3.1 inches

Empire State Building
New York City, NY, USA

designed by
design aus
conçu par
diseñado por
Projetado por
kivitel
Adam Reed Tucker

LEGO Architecture

Empire State Building
New York City, New York, USA

10+
21002

Landmark Series
Wahrzeichen Serie
Série Point de Repère
Serie de la Señal
Série Marco
Mérföldkönek Sorozat

designed by
Adam Reed Tucker

21002

TOY OF THE YEAR AWARDS
TOTY 2013 WINNER

Package design for 21002 Empire State Building.

design of the booklet and instructions, get the box print ready, make the box, bag the bricks, seal the bags and finally seal the box ready for sale. Additionally, Adam was further tasked with securing all of the license agreements, selling and distribution. All these steps had to be fulfilled by Adam and himself alone. He had never taken business classes nor had an interest to, but that did not stop him from spending countless hours at Barnes & Nobel bookstores to research these areas as he had little time to enroll in classes.

This task, although daunting in its very nature, not only gave Adam a more hand-on experience of creating a product, but it also allowed him to learn more about publishing and manufacturing packaging. These skills would help to give him a further understanding of how to apply his design skills as he found himself learning about offset printing, packaging materials, packaging dye, fulfilment, master shipper and all the unknown processes and details that dictates how the final product will look when it is eventually placed on a shelf for sale. It seemed to be a natural step up from creating and sorting the pieces for 250 of your own sets, yet as Adam recalls Paal purposefully had it in mind that the majority of the work had to be on Adam's shoulders alone.

"I had to learn it all on my own. Paal from The LEGO Group had eight other projects to manage and he was in Billund, Denmark, so there was no hand holding. If it was going to be a success then I had to make it happen on my own. That was Paal's model. I truly believed that the Architecture range could happen, so I went out there and I made sure it did." The entrepreneurial spirit began to flourish and thrive as Adam nursed his conviction and belief in his product. Armed with a few demonstration sets and the will to succeed, Adam hit the streets of Chicago in search of a strategically placed gift shop to stock his wares.

After honing in on shops that could be potential retailers, and aiming to target a main demographic and passing trade for the models in question, Adam found a small gift shop that sold Sears Tower's merchandise on Michigan Avenue. He entered into negotiations with the owner about selling his sets in the store. They both agreed to a $19.99 shelf price and initially the store took two cases of 40 sets, on a sale or return basis. It required trust to hand over his stock, the future of the sets were now in the hands of a stranger. Later that night Adam received a phone call from the owner of the gift shop saying that all the stock had been sold. Before the owner could flip his open sign to read closed, his gift shop managed to clear two cases without any promotion, branding or advertising. Adam woke early the next morning and returned back to the city, to restock the store, this time with four cases. It was only 48 hours later that he received another call requesting four more cases and within three days later the gift shop was again sold out.

The rate at which the sets sold was beyond the rate at which Adam could produce them. All 2,500 sets were gone within four working days and yet it took Adam weeks to package them. The demand was overwhelming and Adam could take solace in his findings as he reported the events of the week to The LEGO Group. Needless to say they were more than enthused with the efforts and success of Adam's models, and in response to his hard work they offered to let him keep the profits from the gift shop to pay for his time.

It may have taken weeks of monotonous packing but the proof was evident. There was a demand for a brick-built Architecture range and so far LEGO fans and budding builders could not get enough of it. The LEGO Group was convinced and Adam was called in to discuss the future of Brickstructures. After meetings and negotiations were held, in 2008 The LEGO Group and Adam decided to launch 21000 Sears Tower and 21001 John Hancock Centre as official LEGO Architecture sets. The LEGO Architecture range was born.

It was decided that the sets would be launched in gift shops around Chicago as well as architecture shops on the east and west coast. The first six months proved to be just as successful as the initial run of 2,500 sets, which was then followed by 5,000 sets and then a further 10,000, but after much consideration – and much success – the decision was made to expand upon the range and to leave Adam's local Chicago territory.

Paal settled on the idea of taking an architectural icon on the east and west coast and bringing them into the range to further test the reach of the theme's popularity. The icons chosen were the Empire State Building, to represent the east coast, and the Seattle Space Needle to represent the west. These fitting miniature tributes were chosen because of their imperative importance in the representing east and west-coast architecture. There were also practical implications to consider such as what parts were available, what would make a good keepsakes, and what could be produced and sold for under $20. They not only have wide appeal as souvenir models but they wonderfully reflect the differences between east and west-coast architecture by way of color and form. Again, Adam took to his studio and emerged with accurate and clever interpretations of the chosen buildings. Even though Adam took great pleasure in his craft, and the challenges that creating these miniature brick-built models present, he would continue to push the boundaries of the range. He wanted to explore new territories and sub-themes in a way that may not be conventional, but would inevitably prove Adam's entrepreneurial capabilities and his maverick style approach to his creative vision.

"If it was going to be a success, I had to make it happen on my own"

A rare glimpse of Adam working on LEGO Architecture prototypes.

Kjeld Christiansen the grandson of the the founder takes some build time with Adam.

|WORKING WITH THE LEGO GROUP

21000 SEARS TOWER
Pieces: 69
RRP £17.99 / $19.99 / 19.99€

21002: EMPIRE STATE BUILDING
Pieces: 77
RRP $19.99, £19.99, 19.99€

58 BRICKSCULTURE

LAUNCHING ARCHITECTURE

As momentum for this exciting and unique LEGO theme began to build, Adam started to consider the way in which the Architecture theme could be further developed. Creating famous landmarks and architectural sites provides endless possibilities for sets, but to really engage an audience there needed to be a structured approach to the selection and release of the different models. When reflecting on the popularity of the previous models, Adam realized that he could diversify the appeal of the Architecture range by dividing it into two sub-themes: a Landmark series, which would celebrate famous structures around the world; and an Architect series, which gives the builder a journey through vital architects and their work. Having these two clear divides would go on to benefit the range because it opened up a huge opportunity for revenue streams through licensing agreements with architectural firms. Not surprisingly, Adam wasted no time in going for what he considered to be one of the most successful and widely-recognized architectural masters of our time: Frank Lloyd Wright.

"Our first model in the Architect range had to be a really well known and recognized architect so I went straight to the top and made a small model of Fallingwater by Frank Lloyd Wright, which I

21003: SEATTLE SPACE NEEDLE
Pieces: 57
RRP$19.99, £19.99, 19.99€

21001 JOHN HANCOCK CENTER
Pieces: 69
RRP$19.99

Concept artwork for Adams Coliseum model which didn't make it to market.

LEGO Architecture

The Colosseum
Rome, Italy

Ages/edades
12+
210XX
XXXpcs/pzs

Landmark Series
Série Landmark
Serie Monumental

Model designed by
XXXXXXXXXXXXX

Building Toy
Jouet de Construction
Juguete para Construir

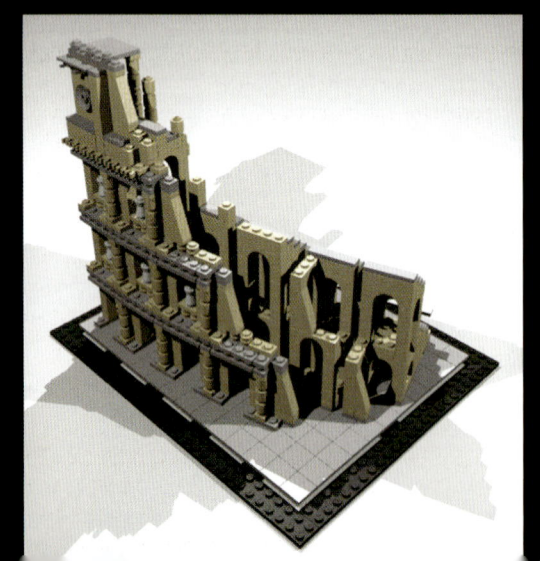

Concept artwork for Eames House.

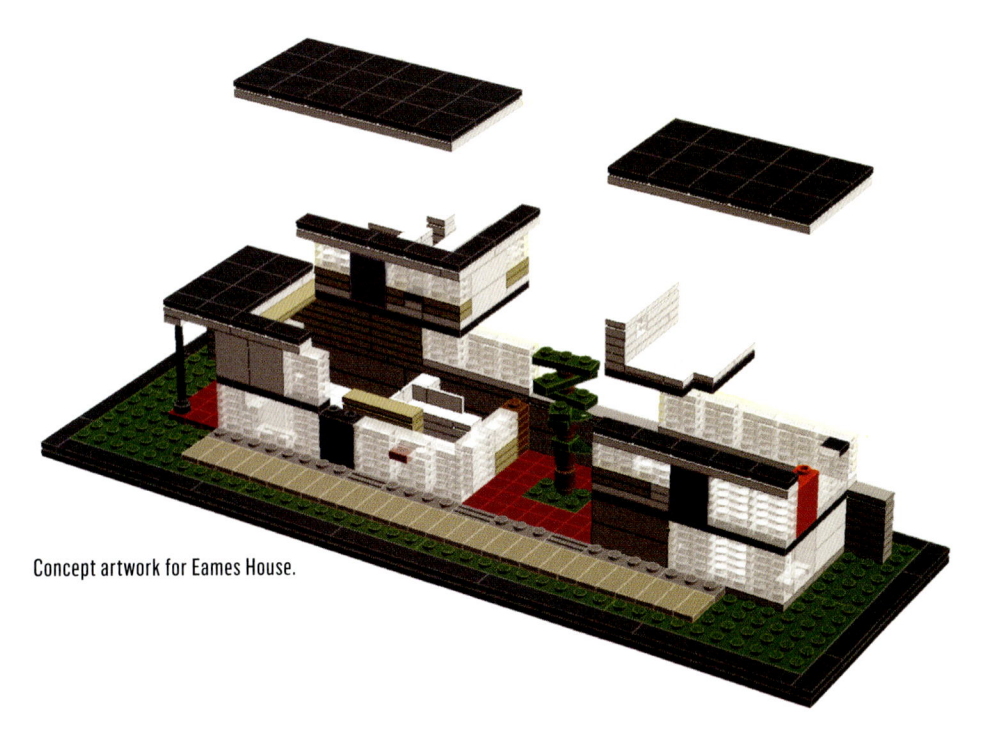

"I truly believed the LEGO Architecture range could happen, so I went out there and made sure that I did"

made by recycling an old Harry Potter castle set because of all the dark tan required to make the model fit the color scheme of Fallingwater." Adam's ambition to aim high continued to manifest: his determination lead him to not only create an accurate representation of the subject matter, but Adam would pitch it in a unique and eccentric way that very few would consider to attempt, let alone try to execute.

Adam traveled with his Fallingwater model to Taliesin, the headquarters of the Frank Lloyd Wright Foundation in Spring Green, Wisconsin, where he had set up a meeting with the foundation's licensing team to discuss a potential licensing deal. The team engaged with the model and saw its potential as a gift but didn't see it as having a mass appeal that was strong enough to warrant creating a series of Frank Lloyd Wright buildings. The meeting may not have gone to plan but with a firm belief in his product and an open discourse with the company, Adam pushed the pitching boundaries to help the board realize the true potential for his new idea. With the feedback from the meeting in mind, Adam wasted no time in heading straight to the Taliesin gift shop, which sold Fallingwater memorabilia and books about Frank Lloyd Wright. In a rather unorthodox and radical stunt, Adam found a piece of merchandise being sold for $34.99 and, when no one was looking, cleared the product off the shelf and replaced it with his Fallingwater LEGO model, adding the $34.99 price tag.

Adam then called the Director of the licensing team and told him to meet him on the gift shop premises for a further discussion, to which he agreed. Whilst Adam waited for the Director to arrive he discreetly wandered the gift shop observing all the merchandise keeping his eyes peeled to make sure the staff hadn't disturbed the planted model. With a stroke of luck the director arrived promptly as did of a group of tourists who took to looking around the shop. With a quick confession of what he had planted, the Director played the part of the onlooker and the two waited for tourists to interact with the model. It didn't take long for a few of the tourists to notice the model and start to take interest. After taking an interest, but unable to find any packaged products, one of the tourists took the model over to the checkout and asked where they could find a boxed version of the model. The cashier may have been confused about the model, but the Director of Licensing certainly wasn't. "He looked at me and said 'you're crazy, but I love it.'" Before inviting Adam back into his office to sign the first LEGO Architect licensing deal.

A stunt of that magnitude may have been a huge risk to take but with complete faith in the product, Adam was willing to do the extraordinary and went back to The LEGO Group with a signed licensing contract. What is perhaps more astonishing about the "crazy" stunt was that Adam had planned, prepared and executed this idea without informing The LEGO Group at all. The way Adam saw it, he wasn't working for The LEGO Group but rather working with The LEGO Group on LEGO Architecture, so heading back with a signed licensing agreement was nothing but a step in the

"I went straight to the top and made a small model of Fallingwater by Frank Lloyd Wright, which I made by recycling an old Harry Potter castle"

right direction to bringing more success to the range. Adam regaled the story to Paal at The LEGO Group who thought the whole story was utter brilliance. A new discussion opened on how to populate the Architect sub-themes within LEGO Architecture and three structures made the cut: Frank Lloyd Wright's Fallingwater, his Solomon R. Guggenheim Museum and Frederick C. Robie House. With Paal sourcing any and all parts that Adam required to create these models, Adam now found himself building without restrictions as he took on the role of LEGO Designer for the Architecture range. One of the major benefits to working as a designer wasn't just the increased availability in parts but also the ability to request elements in any of the existing color palettes and even, on the rare occasion where extreme necessity required, a brand new element.

With his own home studio now fully equipped and a list of models that needed to be built, Adam embarked on creating the models that make up the LEGO Architecture range. The intense creative endeavor and a rough time scale of two months to create each model, meant no time could be wasted waiting for colored parts to arrive. This hindered the artist and gave Adam a barrier when designing the likes of the Prairie-School-style Robie House, for which no dark red parts were currently in circulation, and Fallingwater, which required a few Star Wars elements in tan to be added for complete accuracy. To overcome this obstacle Adam decided to start building using a new technique familiar to him from his early days of designing buildings using wood. With an interest in not relying on new parts to arrive and to help gain a better understanding of form without getting lost in color, Adam began to build all his models in grayscale. By only using grey bricks it meant he didn't have to worry about color scheme until later on in the design process, and instead could focus all his time dedicated to the true form of the building, how the light hits its surface and how it's viewed from multiple angles. As a designer, this became an imperative part of Adam's creative process and creating first drafts in a single tone is a practice he still follows today, regardless of the scale of the build.

As well as desaturating his builds, Adam employed other techniques from his days as an architect including his process for researching and understanding his subject matter. His library of architecture books, journals and magazines would come back into his life to prove their worth as, before even touching a brick, Adam would focus on familiarizing himself with every aspect, angle and detail of his chosen subject. As any scale builder will tell you, having different reference materials for your subject can more often than not provide an invaluable resource when faced with a design flaw or build problem to solve.

Through his process of extensive research and desaturation, Adam successfully designed more than 40 potential models, some of which were put forward by himself and some of which were requested by The LEGO Group. The range developed in a way that saw it become transcontinental, moving from American icons to European landmarks and even making its way to Australia with the likes of the Sydney Opera House. Within three years of designing for The LEGO Group, Adam had created 15 official models as well as contributed to the widely-appreciated LEGO architecture studio: a box containing only white elements and a comprehensive guide to building architecture which will inspire even the most seasoned builder.

By 2012, Adam had single-handedly developed an entire LEGO theme based around his passion for architecture, which to this day still has mass appeal to builders of all ages and each year continues to see more structures immortalized in LEGO sets. From drilling his own bricks, selling sets himself, planning risky stunts to impress prospective clients and then spending countless hours painstakingly crafting models, by his own initiative and determination Adam took his small idea and made it an absolute success.

The romance of the LEGO Architecture range and Adam Reed Tucker would not be one that lasted forever, however. Come 2012 a change in The LEGO Group's mandates for outsourcing and contracting stated that all work across The LEGO Group must be streamlined, which meant only using internal designers to create new sets. With a congratulatory farewell and a 'thank you for all the hard work', Adam and LEGO Architecture parted ways. After an incredible journey, having created an outstanding portfolio and innumerable LEGO contacts, Adam was free to reinvent himself and to start new ventures under his prestigious titles of LEGO Certified Professional and founder of LEGO Architecture.

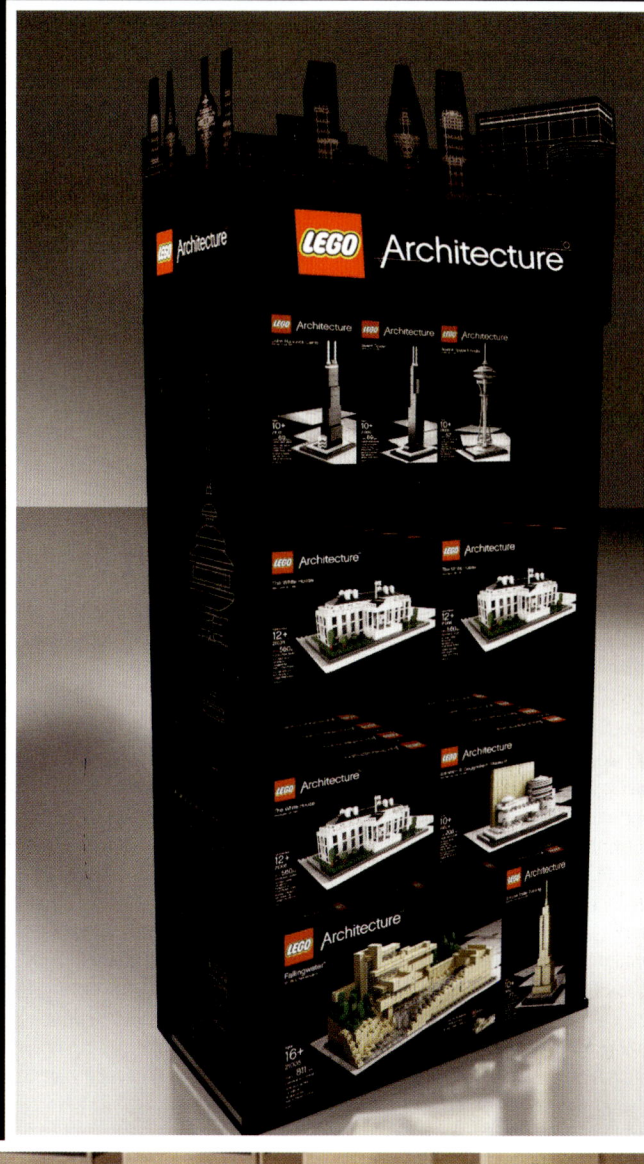

This first official batch of LEGO Architecture sets fresh off the assembly line and ready for sale.

BRICKWORLD BEGINNINGS

BUILDING EVENTS

Now that Adam had closed his chapter on LEGO Architecture and left the realms of design for The LEGO Group behind him, it was time to get back to creating and earning under his prestigious LEGO Certified Professional status. Looking back to 2012, before his first meeting with Tormod and Paal, Adam had two major strings to his bow: his ability to create complex and artistic sculptures of architecture; and his knowledge of event organizing gained from setting up Brickworld in Chicago. It's the latter that we look back on here as a springboard for creating his future exhibits and business.

His initial drive to Brickfest Washington in 2006 was a gruelling 15-hour straight drive in an unair-conditioned rental van, with terrible suspension, in mid-August. Not only were the circumstances of the drive uncomfortable and unforgiving on the driver, but the sheer distance traveled across American roads meant that all of Adam's eight models arrived resembling something different to what they started the journey as. It was nine o'clock when he arrived but after re-building his models it was 2am, giving the artist little time to rest before the show began. During the last day of the show, fellow AFOL Bryan Bonahoom asked if he enjoyed the show and Adam's response was honest but oxymoronic: "Yes I loved the show, it was brilliant. But, I'm never coming back again." After the long and cumbersome drive to the venue, having to reassemble his models, spending the long weekend interacting with people, striping his buildings and leaving the show, the last thing Adam wanted to do was another 15-hour drive only to find his buildings in disarray on arrival home. By the time he reached his home in Chicago he could say with absolute conviction that it was an experience he did not want to repeat. Those who have transported a LEGO model over any distance will know the precocious and delicate nature driving a car becomes. It certainly adds an extra stress and extra energy into travelling, and Adam wouldn't have it. There must be a closer alternative. Desperate to show his wares, Adam reached out to his newfound community to try to find a closer alternative but his call was not met with much joy.

Determined not travel all that way again, and the chance to seize a gap in the market, Adam came back to the community and asked who, if anyone, wanted to join forces with him to help build an event in Chicago. At first Adam's request was met with interest in participating in a Chicago event, but no-one seemed to share Adam's initiative and desire to create and manage it. Silence was deafening, and the artist started to fear that he may be creating, funding and hosting an event by himself. The call was finally answered by none-other than Indianapolis LEGO fan Bryan Bonahoom, the same Bryan who discussed and agreed with the shortcomings of the Washington event. Bryan met with Adam to discuss what each of them could bring to the party, as well as the details such as venue, crowd sizes, exhibitors and most importantly the finances needed to make the show a success. Adam took the initiative in naming and promoting the show, as well as using his LCP status to get LEGO to support the event, whereas Bryan had the AFOL contacts to populate the event and more experience with attending shows, thus the expectation of how a successful event should be ran. With no sponsors but still the need to secure a venue, it was up to Adam and Bryan to fund the show themselves. However, once the cash was secured and a lot of hard work, Brickworld was formed and Bryan reached out to engage with the AFOL community.

"Bryan was the window to the community" says Adam. "We needed support and visitors because I didn't know anyone. Being the socialite that he is, Bryan started reaching out and talking to everybody in the local and extended community, and that's how we got 200 exhibitors the first year and now we have more than 1,000." With Adam acting as the catalyst and LEGO agent, and Bryan organizing and running the show, Brickworld successfully snowballed from 20,000 square feet, 250 exhibitors and 4,000 attendees to 100,000 square feet, 1,000 exhibitors and 15,000 attendees. The available platform has given countless LEGO fans the chance to display their creations to the public, and has opened its doors to the residents of Chicago for inspiration, entertainment and enjoyment every June.

Adam had two main motives for founding Brickworld: his desire to have a show closer to home; and to provide other builders with a platform to display their art. By 2011, six years after forming Brickworld, Adam's time was becoming increasingly scarce with his traveling exhibitions and his work for The LEGO Group. He began to find it increasingly difficult to dedicate time to the running and organizing of Brickworld but, in contrast, Bryan found himself wanting to dedicate even more time to the Brickworld cause. He was even on the brink of giving up his day job to organize the show full time. After all, when you have over 15,000 members of the public coming through your door and an increasing demand for three more annual events, you find yourself with an operation that needs full-time support and dedication all year round. Adam saw how much Bryan wished to grow the show and decided that his work with Brickworld had come to an end. The two decided that Bryan would take full control of the event and he continues to take Brickworld from strength to strength.

Adam and Bryan parted ways and Adam put his models into his traveling exhibition full time. As the artist recollects, it was a good natured and natural departure from the partnership: "My work was done. I'm very good at developing an idea and starting projects, but once they have success and stability I get bored, and seek other creative endeavours." Just like his work with LEGO Architecture, Adam left with the most valuable thing – a positive mental attitude and a strong conviction in his creative talents. With that he returned to his life of being an LCP and creating new business ideas as well as commissioned work and exhibitions. The legacy of Brickworld continues as thanks to the will of Adam and Bryan, builders' young and old from all over Illinois and the surrounding states have a platform they can use to exhibit their work.

"For me it was mostly about giving something back to the community," says Adam. "Brickfest gave me a platform, Brickworld gave me a chance to pass on that torch and give a platform to somebody else. That's all there was to it."

Brickworld 2007

Adam at Brickworld with Tormod, Kjeld, Jorgen and Bryan.

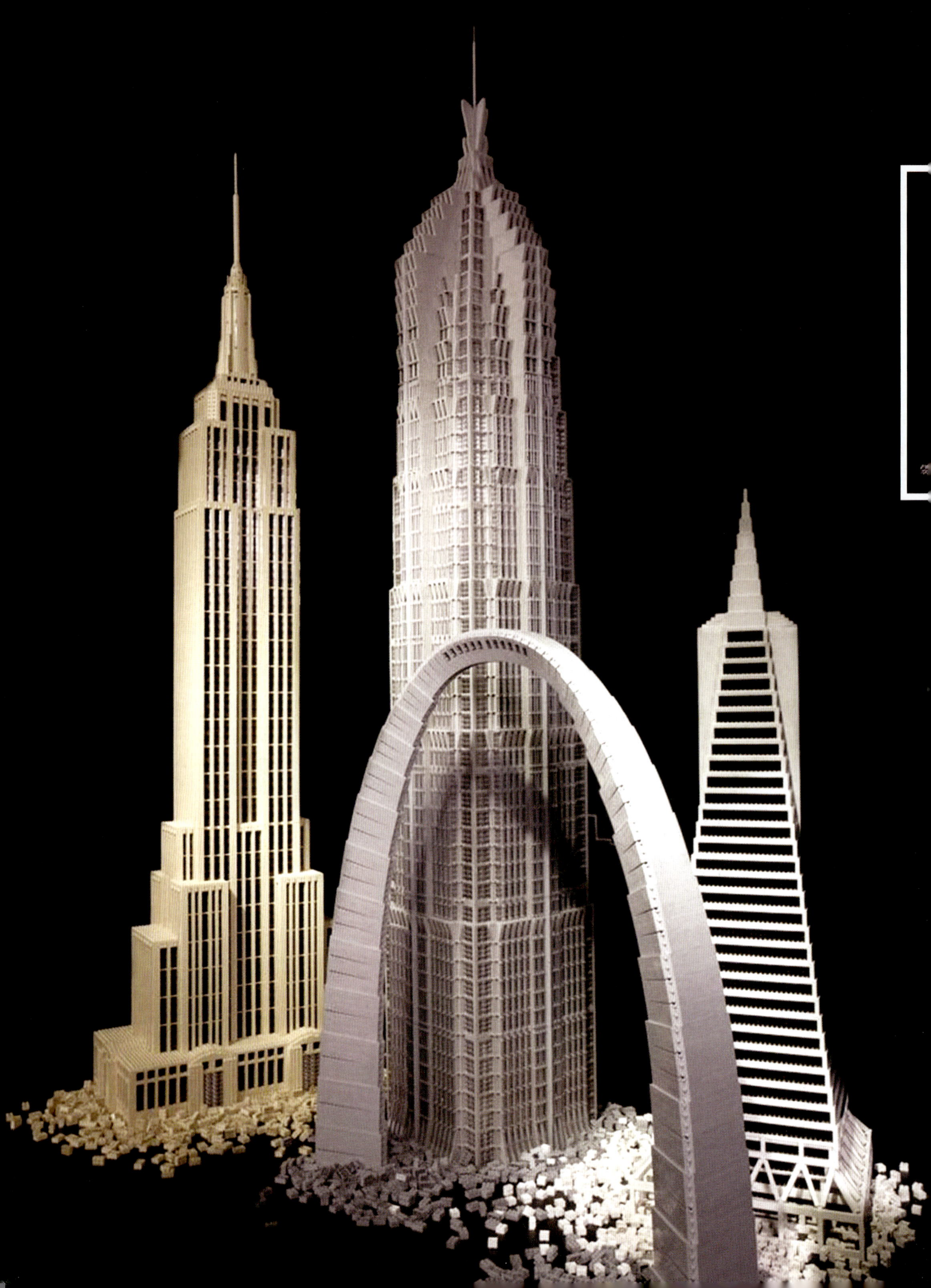

GOING BEYOND

At the same time as creating his own range of LEGO models, Adam continued his drive to become a recognized artist and change the way LEGO construction was perceived by hitting the road and taking his touring exhibition across North America

To entertain the full-time commitment of single handily designing a new LEGO range is an opportunity that few have been given, let alone making a success of. Combine that with the underlying part-time commitment to put together a show such as Brickworld and suddenly your calendar starts to become rather populated and time management becomes vital. Combine that with creating your own structures that you curate into an exhibit, which you then have to sell to clients, manage, deliver and set up at the venue without any external help, and you can begin to see how Adam Reed Tucker went from a determined creative individual to a professional and thriving artist. His traveling exhibitions provided a gentle background to the rest of his work in 2007, however by 2012 it would go from strength to strength to become a flourishing creative endeavor.

The transition from a starving artist to a thriving one can be a very romanticized way to view the artistic life, and there are very few who can do little work and go onto achieve overnight success. In the words of the famous American comedian Eddie Cantor: "It takes 20 years to become an overnight success." So how are those 20 years filled? In Adam's case it was the constant exploration of different creative avenues without the worry of success or failure. The only goal in mind was the desire to inspire and enable others to create – if that is achieved then the project is a success – and with that came an audience, and with the audience came monetization. Until this point of having a dedicated audience, it was up to Adam to front the costs of exhibiting himself, and once he began to create exhibits outside of the local scene the financial payoff was little compared to the work involved. The story is one that many artists will know, and it is a predicament that drives many to financial and emotional exhaustion.

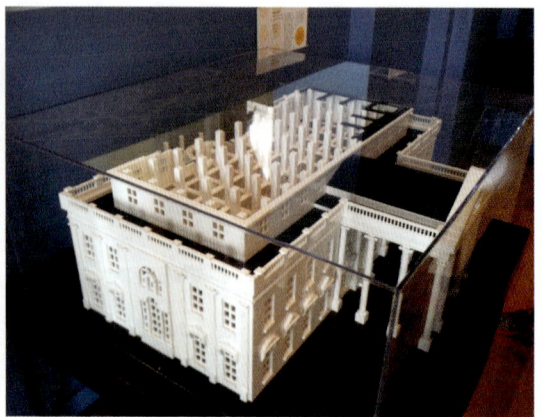

"As a starving artist you begin by willing to set up for free... the reality is that I was actually paying money to set up"

"My first exhibit away from a LEGO show was at a little discovery center and when I set it up there I was paid a very small sum. As a starving artist you begin by willing to set up for free...the reality is that I was actually paying money to set up," says Adam. It's a conundrum that most artists go through, and Adam had certainly had his share of pay-to-display experiences, such as Brickfest in Washington. The struggle is that there is no method or progression path you can follow in order to achieve artistic success, a term which by its very nature changes depending on the person seeking the status. The basics come down to application: if you're an artist create art, if you're a painter paint, if you're a writer write or if you're a singer then sing. The problem artists' face is the monetization that enables them to live off their art. So how did Adam go from getting a small fee to set up, to getting paid ten times that to set up his work for display? By nurturing his artistic will and employing business accruement that would monetize his art, a practice that is perfectly exemplified by his traveling exhibitions.

After Brickfest and Brickworld Adam realized that he had enough sculptures to be able to offer venues a unique exhibition about architecture using a universally engaging medium: the LEGO brick. The interaction he had received at shows from members of the public gave Adam the confidence to approach the Discovery Center Museum in Rockford and pitch his models as a viable candidate for a special exhibition. Accepting a small fee Adam set up his models for a three-month tenancy with the hope of stoking interest for other larger exhibition venues. Rockford may have been a small and humble venue but, as it was the artist's first public exhibition outside of the LEGO community sphere, Adam made sure that the models were organized, arranged and presented in a stylish and considered manner. Even though the exhibition put very little into Adam's pocket, and it can be argued that the museum made more off his work than he did, the exhibition successfully drew the attention of a much larger, and much more prestigious, venue in the form of The Museum of Science and Industry in Chicago.

After its six-month residency at The Museum of Science and Industry, word caught on about the complex and magnificent LEGO Architecture exhibition and the popularity of the exhibition began to snowball. From the Museum of Science and Industry, it was picked up by the National Building Museum in Washington for a year-long tenancy. In that year, numbers of visitors to the museum increased and it proved to be one of the most successful exhibitions in the National Building Museum to date. As a result the board requested to extend the exhibition for another year and for the first time charged a separate entrance fee to see Adam's work, opening up a huge revenue stream opportunity for the museum and artist.

Once its two-year residency at the National Building Museum came to a close, Adam had financial reports and hard evidence that bringing his exhibition to a venue would

BRICKS CULTURE 69

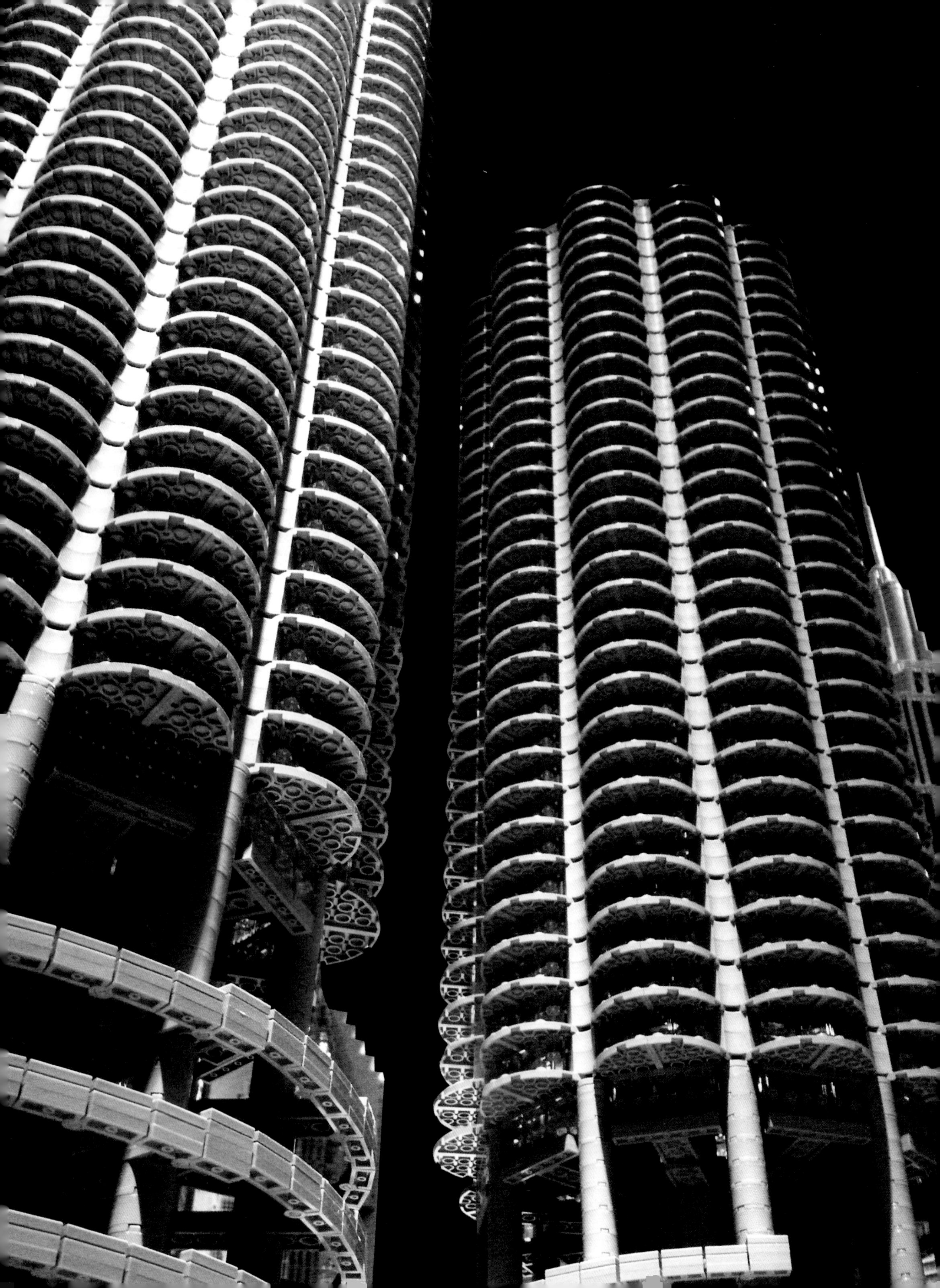

not only increase visitor numbers, but it could potentially open up brand new revenue streams. The exhibition refused to lay dormant, as after the National Building Museum's tenancy was up it traveled to the Henry Ford Museum for a year. Next, the exhibit found itself renamed as 'Icons of the Sky: LEGO Architecture' at Midland Center for the Arts in Michigan. This signaled a shift in the way in which Adam's models could be viewed, as rather than being housed in a museum environment they found themselves for the first time as an art installation. Then it found itself rebranded as 'Dream It Build It' at the Grand Rapids Public Museum in Michigan. Leaving its tour of Michigan, the exhibition went to Gail Borden Public Library in Elgin and then Arlington Heights Public Library, where the exhibit found itself in a completely different situation, location and layout than before. From the library setting, it morphed and returned to its art exhibit layout at the Figge Art Museum in Davenport, and then back to where Adam went to College in Kansas City at the aptly-named The Box Gallery. From the gallery it went to Imagination Station in Ohio where it was rebranded as 'Sky High Science' and there it currently resides, but there is no doubt that it will continue to tour and prove successful for many other venues in the future.

The secret to creating an exhibition that could be housed in many different kinds of venue runs far deeper than the reports of the financial benefits that it could bring to the building that housed it. Adam's sculptures provided an engaging stimuli using a universally recognized medium which could be used as a means to promote creativity, learn about industry and learn about architecture and construction. They enable people to learn about architecture as an art form, about engineering, and bring community teams and LEGO builders together. The sculptors can even provide their own backdrop to be appreciated as works of art. The versatility of this way of thinking, as well as the quality and quantity of the models themselves, play a huge role in the success of the exhibition as a whole. With the scope to use the form of Adam's models to provide different functions, the models can be toured constantly whilst keeping a unique tone and thus an open revenue stream with constant monetization options.

Every exhibit has had similar models, and yet every exhibit has had a different name, focus and theme around the subject matter they wanted to explore. The process begins with a meeting between Adam and the venue's creative team where a discussion is had on how the venue's team wishes to portray and organize the space. It's important that any particular objectives or expectations for the exhibit are brought to the table as once a firm grasp of theme, tone and layout is decided the team can rapidly move forward in bringing all the unique graphics and assets together to fill the space. It's an incredibly organic and collaborative process that provides a solid basis from which to start the exhibition. Here Adam can make the most of his LCP status and bring in bulk bricks for interactive stands and organized

TRAVELLING EXHIBITS

activities, one of which is the inspirational 'City of Tomorrow'. As Adam recollects it's an activity that provides attendants the rare opportunity to work as he does.

"We brought in two dozen K8 boxes, which contain thousands of white bricks and plates, and everyone pitched in to create a huge monochromatic diorama." As you may recollect Adam sees working with a single color as the best way to build as it allows you to focus entirely on form rather than worrying about getting the color right. Not only did the 'City of Tomorrow' allow the participants to take on this element of Adam's build style but it also familiarized them with the limited nature of building LEGO Architecture sets, as each participant was given just five bricks which could be added to existing structures to made into their own. As long as they weren't removing bricks that others had placed they could add to the city, which really allowed them to explore what it's like to add their own touch to an existing area, and work in a condition where every brick placement is vital. The city was filmed expanding over three months and played at the exhibit, which added to the theme and the overall tone of the exhibition.

Even though Adam's work is architecturally focused, the theme of the exhibition wasn't strictly an appreciation of architecture. The Museum of Science and Industry, for instance, decided on the educational Art + Science = Architecture whereas the National Building Museum took the inspirational tone of called it 'Towering Ambition'. With the change in focus, came the change in the presentation of the sculptures, which in turn increased the unique selling point of each exhibition. The majority of the venues had the models as the centerpieces but then

"I've aged ten years and the exhibit has not. It took around four hours to set up originally, now it takes around six"

employed carefully considered backdrops, quotations and facts to merge the tone of the exhibition to their desired theme. In contrast to the thematic exhibition style of approach, The Box Gallery and Midland Art Museum opt for a more minimalist approach where the pieces were on display in a plain room with plenty of space to breathe and be observed. This gave a different perspective with which the onlooker could enjoy Adam's creations and a different setting, which presented his work as singular works of art. There was no running narrative through the exhibition, the models themselves were left to tell the story. To create a more live and interactive exhibition feel, the Discovery Science Center arranged the sculptures in one room with quotes and narratives across the walls. The combination of sculptures and quotes were intended to inspire visitors to go into breakout rooms and create based on what they had seen and experienced. Each exhibit used similar models, and yet each provided a unique way to enjoy them.

One thing that stayed the same throughout every exhibition, though, was that all the models were delivered, set up, taken down and transported to the next location by Adam and Adam alone. "It's natural that you tend to forget things when you are not active with them, but by setting them up myself I'm kept connected to my art," he says. This becomes evident if you head down to one of the artist's exhibitions on set-up day. There are no huge barriers or curtains sealing off the area, there is no grand unveiling of pre-assembled sculptures. The space is left open and free so that visitors can see how Adam assembles his models by hand, in a modest t-shirt and shorts, sweating and endeavoring to assemble the art that makes up his exhibit. What is even more remarkable than the artist's modesty is his complex knowledge of each model which not only makes it quicker for him to set everything up, but practically means he is the only person who could assemble the models. As Adam explains: "Since I don't use any glue they are all very fragile. There are no steel armatures inside, so the pieces have to be hand packed and hand erected for every show, I'm the only one that really could assemble them." As the lucky spectators of Adam's set-up would know, each of his models have around six different sections

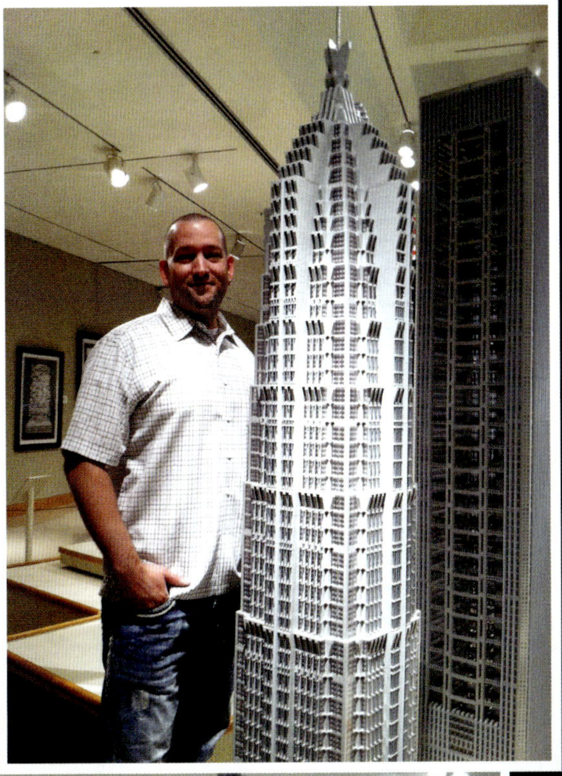

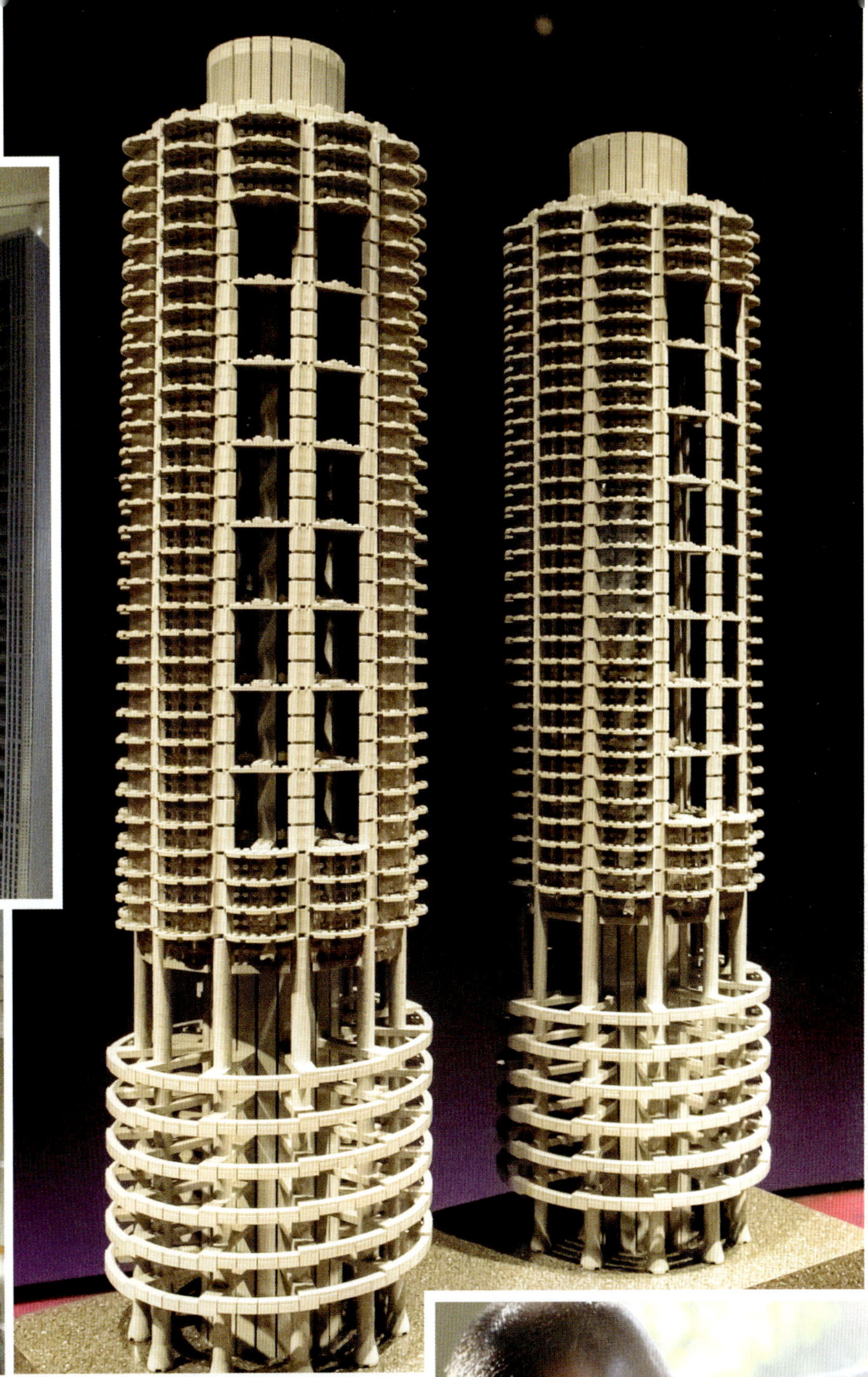

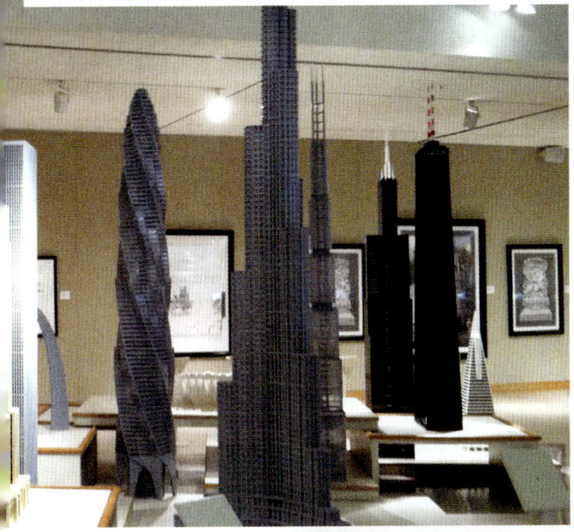

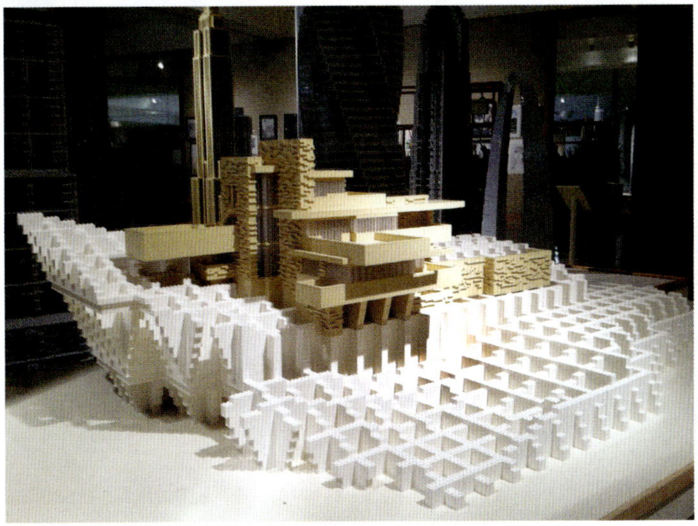

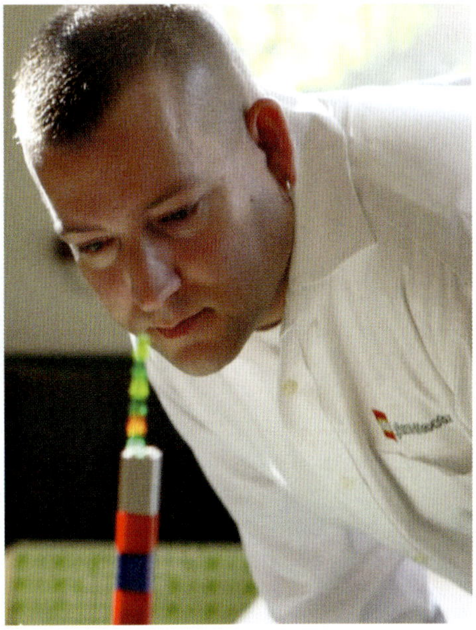

| TRAVELLING EXHIBITS

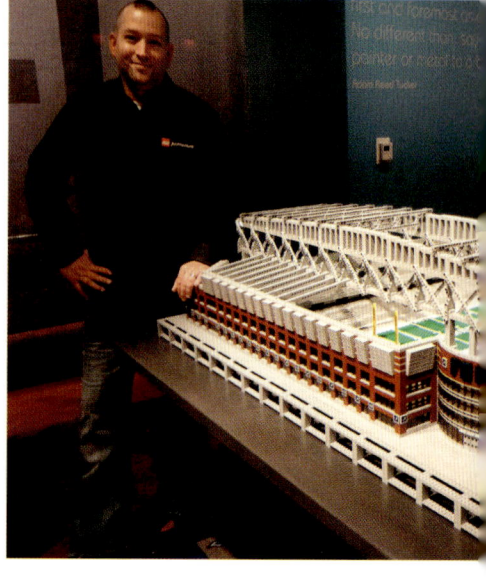

> We have all spent hours sprawled on the floor playing with toy blocks and built little houses with LEGO bricks or some other construction toy. We have all been little architects.
> Witold Rybczynski

Right: Paal Smith-Meyer and Christian Thor-Larson of the LEGO company's new business group (NBG) join Adam at his first east coast exhibit launch at the National Building Museum.

"We brought in two dozen K8 boxes, which contain thousands of white bricks and plates, and everyone pitched in to create a huge monochromatic diorama"

to them, each with their own specific and unique grab points. Grab the section correctly and the assembly will be smooth and fast, but grab the section incorrectly and the entire section risks being destroyed, and your evening will quickly turn from preparing for the media day to re-building an entire section of a model. Although every possible technique can be employed to make erecting and striking as easy as possible, damage and re-assembly – even the smallest off-sections – will always be inevitable. There will always be vibrations during transportation, loose bricks at the bottom of containers and broken sections to deal with, but it's all part of the process that Adam uses to prove that he is the artist. He is the creator of these impressive sculptures and the only person who can reassemble them if broken. Your expert builder may be able to reassemble in time, but when time is constantly against you and you have a mere few hours to complete installation, a complete knowledge of the complex structures is vital. There are no instructions, no computer design to rebuild them, no magic tricks, just an ordinary guy with complete familiarity of his creations.

In 10 years the only thing that has changed about Adam's process is the set-up time, which as Adam notes is only due to his age. "I've aged 10 years, and the exhibit has not. It took around four hours to set up originally, now it takes around six." Which is still rather impressive given the size and magnitude of the models that make up the exhibition. What's more, once he is finished assembling his models it's typical of him to help the museums staff set up any interactive elements, brick pits or build rooms ready for the press weekend launch. All that's left to do once set-up is completed is attend the press launch and artist signing session, as well as the presentations Adam gives where he talks about his story and process so that others can be inspired and encouraged to create. There is no lavish crew, assistants or directors, just a normal man working hard to provide a raw insight into making the most of your creativity. It provides a level of authenticity which is unmatched by other artist exhibitions and provides exceeding value to the venue that houses it.

Even though there are time pressures and physical strain that come with setting and striking everything yourself, it all pays off when Adam meets attendees and comes face to face with his audience. "I really enjoy visiting new destinations but what I enjoy most is sharing my work with an audience who I can interact with afterwards. To see people inspired makes everything worthwhile."

The passion and love that Adam puts into his work is completely evident when you observe his interaction with visitors. There is a genuine and authentic nature about his conversation, which absorbs you just as much as his models do. You can't help but be inspired by him and the honest story he is trying to tell through his models. It makes you want to go home, strip all your LEGO models and start looking at your bricks in a different way. What's more, it isn't just LEGO fans who find themselves inspired by the exhibits. As it's thematically routed in inspiration and education, the only kind of person it needs to inspire is the viewer. Regardless of their walk in life, anyone who attends the exhibit can take something away from it. The LEGO Brick is simply the tool that takes the unfamiliar and makes it the subject you have known for your entire life. It speaks to adults and children in the same way and tells them that they can make anything from their imagination, but it lays the foundations and stimulates you to absorb new information that you may not have taken an interest in before. That is what the exhibition is all about, an artist using a familiar medium to depict familiar subject matters in a way that is completely original and unique. That is where the inspiration comes from – the viewer is motivated to think outside the box and to persevere with their creativity. Everything in the exhibit was made by one man who had an idea, what could your idea achieve?

| LEGO ARCHITECTURE

ARCHITECTURE
CREATING A NEW EXPERIENCE

The beauty of LEGO Architecture is that not only did it build bigger ambitions for LEGO sets, but it offered a creative and intellectual experience for builders around the world. Here are a few sets that made the range so incredibly popular...

LEGO Architecture not only challenged the convention of a LEGO sets' subject matter, but they offer a completely different experience to builders around the world. Rather than the excitement of breaking open a box and building a model with the ultimate aim of play, LEGO Architecture treats its audience to a more academic venture and a different form of gratification.

The sleek and smooth matte black boxes invite you to open them and admire their contents, packaging and booklet, which are assembled with the same keen eye for style that is defined and exemplified by the models in the range. Even the instruction booklet seduces the reader by giving them more than they would expect from a traditional instruction booklet. It's eloquent pages take you through beautiful images and facts about the subject matter, which help bring the set to life and give you a wider appreciation and understanding of the build experience you are about to embark on. Once the model is completed, it serves as a unique reminder of an incredible piece of architecture or a place once visited, all represented through the iconic brick. The gratification comes with every glance, and every time someone takes notice of its elegance. It allows you to create your own piece of art.

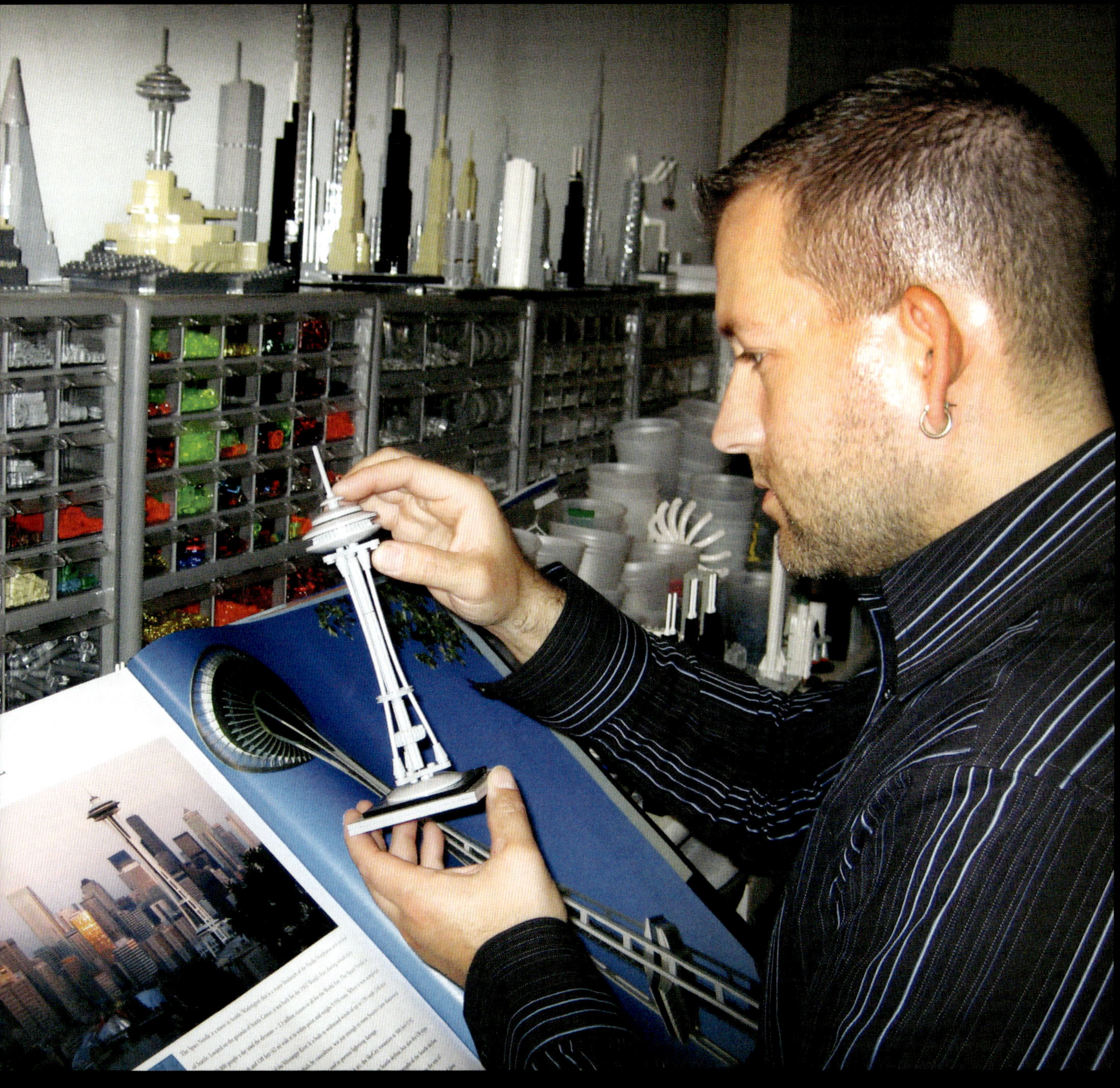

Architecture
Architecture
TECHNIC
TECHNIC
CREATOR

FRANK LLOYD WRIGHT
VISITOR CENTER
ENTRANCE

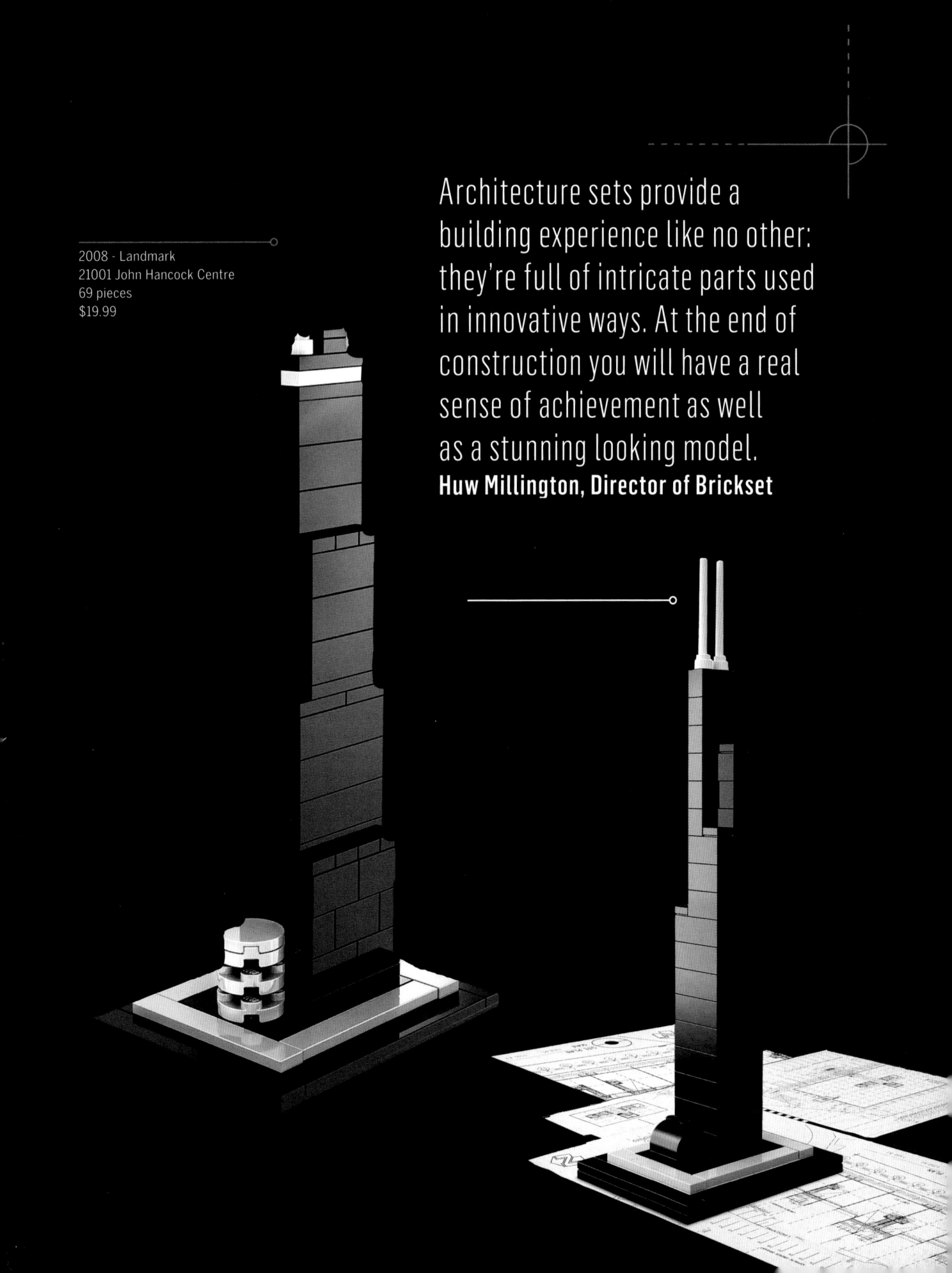

2008 - Landmark
21001 John Hancock Centre
69 pieces
$19.99

Architecture sets provide a building experience like no other: they're full of intricate parts used in innovative ways. At the end of construction you will have a real sense of achievement as well as a stunning looking model.
Huw Millington, Director of Brickset

The series is a way to celebrate an art people encounter everyday, architecture, in a form most know how to handle, the LEGO brick.
Architectural Record

2009 - Landmark
21002 Empire State Building
77 pieces
$19.99

2009 - Landmark
21003 Seattle Space Needle
57 pieces
$19.99

2009 - Architect
21004 Solomon R. Guggenheim Museum
208 pieces
$39.99

Fallingwater was recognized for a design award in 2010 by Wallpaper

2009 - Architect
21005 Fallingwater
811 pieces
$99.99

2010 - Architect
21006 The White House
560 pieces
$49.99

LEGO Architecture

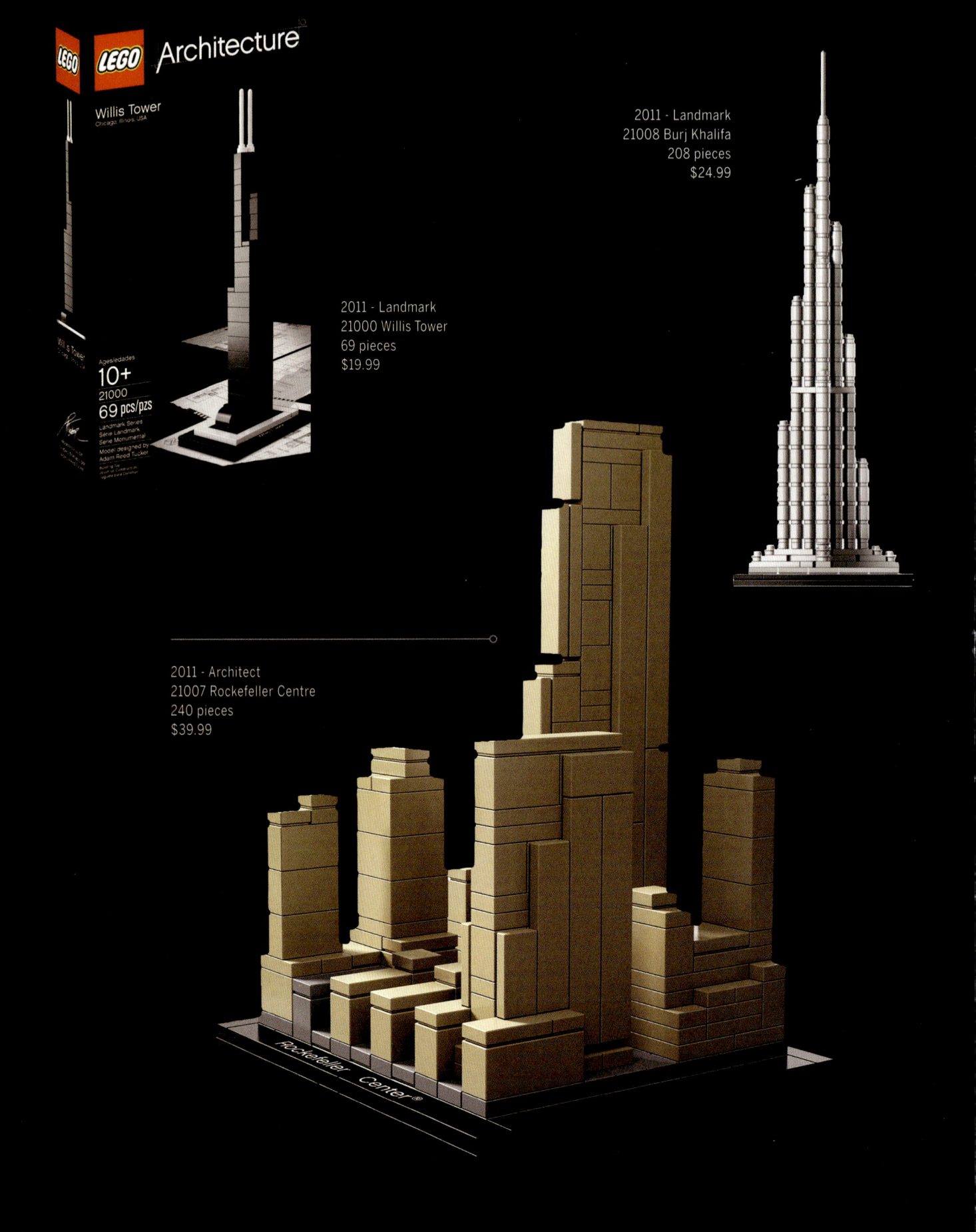

Willis Tower
Chicago, Illinois, USA

2011 - Landmark
21000 Willis Tower
69 pieces
$19.99

2011 - Landmark
21008 Burj Khalifa
208 pieces
$24.99

2011 - Architect
21007 Rockefeller Centre
240 pieces
$39.99

82 BRICKSCULTURE

2011 - Architect
21009 Farnsworth House
546 pieces
$59.99

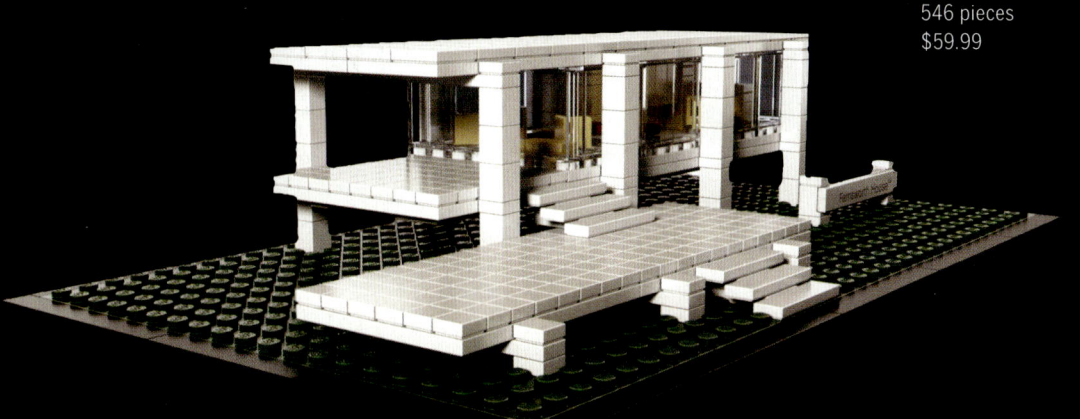

It is designed to free up the imagination, to break your creative preconceptions
Huffington Post

2011 - Architect
21010 Robie House
2276 pieces
$199.99

2011 - Landmark
21011 Brandenburg Gate
363 pieces
$34.99

BRICKSCULTURE 83

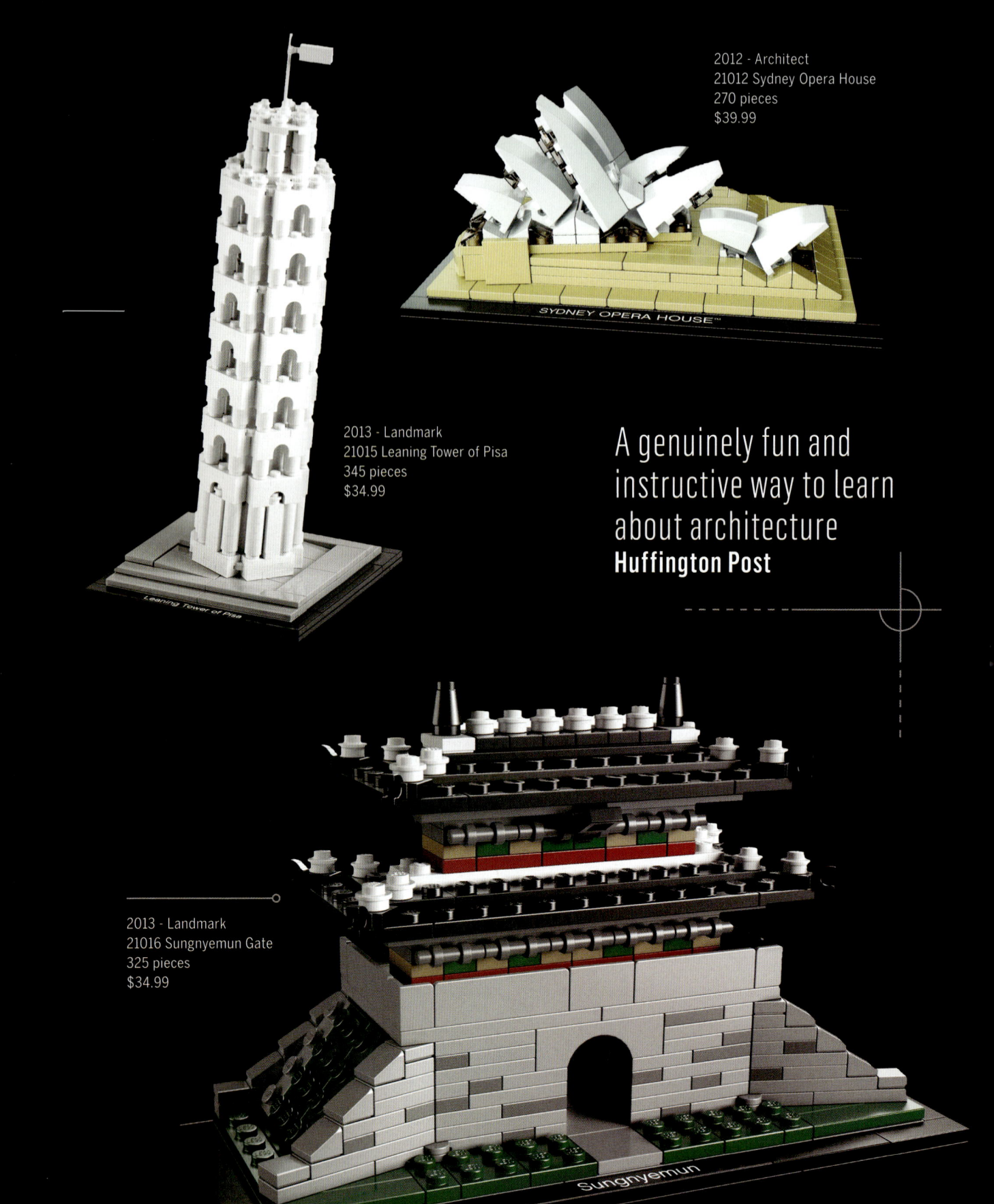

2012 - Architect
21012 Sydney Opera House
270 pieces
$39.99

2013 - Landmark
21015 Leaning Tower of Pisa
345 pieces
$34.99

A genuinely fun and instructive way to learn about architecture
Huffington Post

2013 - Landmark
21016 Sungnyemun Gate
325 pieces
$34.99

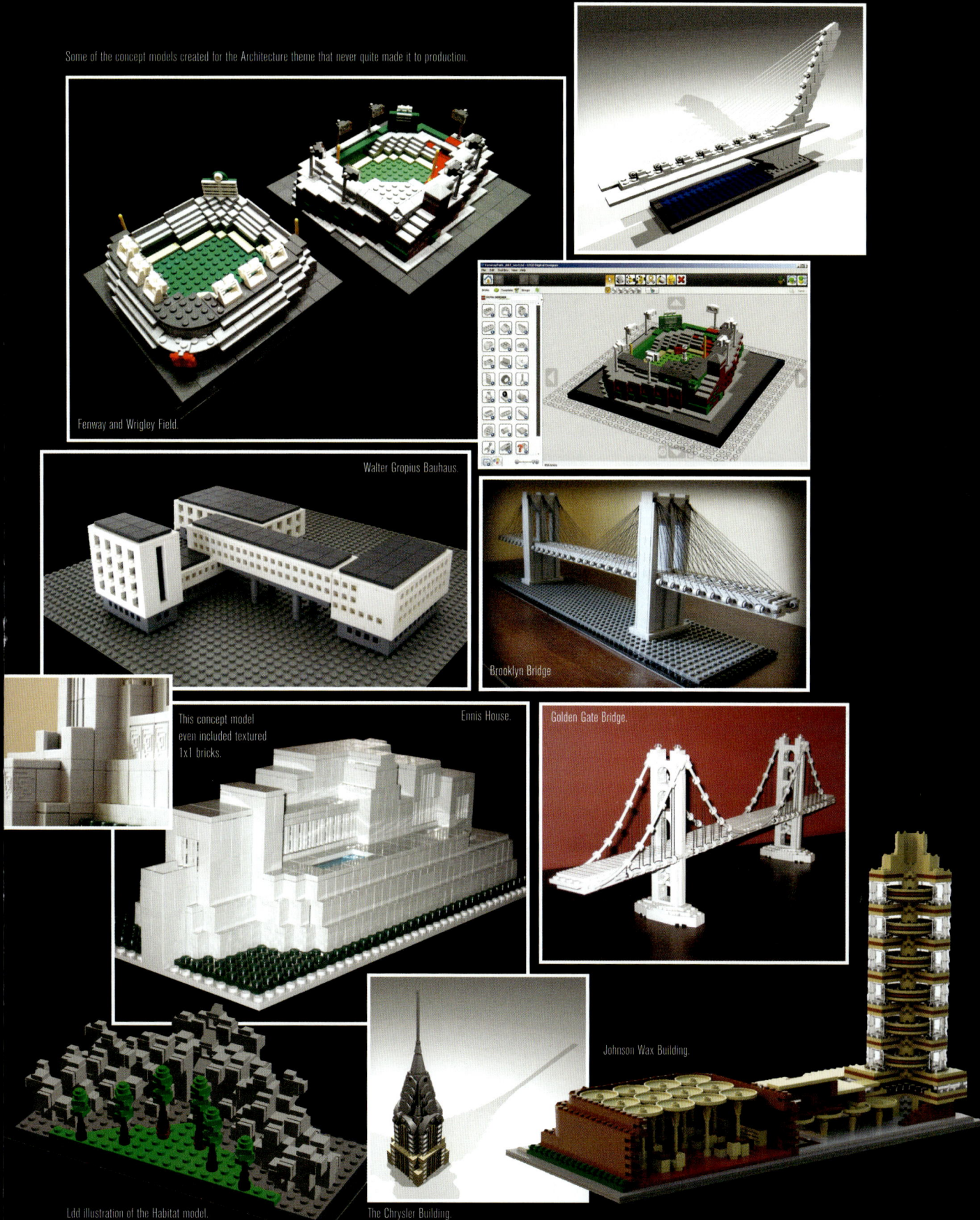

Some of the concept models created for the Architecture theme that never quite made it to production.

Fenway and Wrigley Field.

Walter Gropius Bauhaus.

Brooklyn Bridge.

This concept model even included textured 1x1 bricks.

Ennis House.

Golden Gate Bridge.

Johnson Wax Building.

Ldd illustration of the Habitat model.

The Chrysler Building.

A LEGO EDUCATION

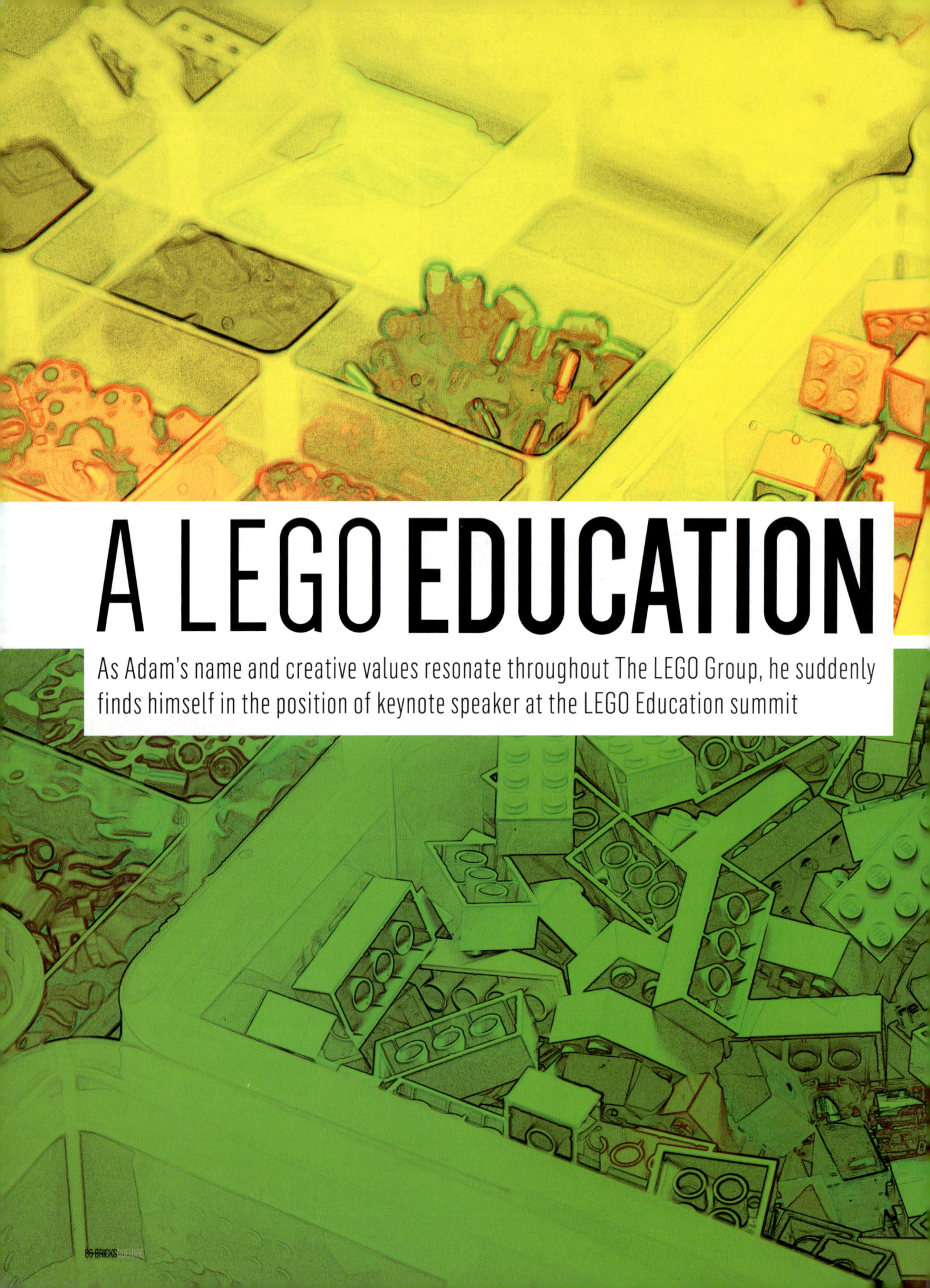

As Adam's name and creative values resonate throughout The LEGO Group, he suddenly finds himself in the position of keynote speaker at the LEGO Education summit

Though Adam and The LEGO Group parted ways in 2012 after the company brought all set designer work in-house, The LEGO Group were still keen to keep Adam close to the brand to benefit from his creative outlook. From the moment The LEGO Group met the artist, it was keen to utilize Adam's unique view of LEGO bricks and their potential to be used to foster education through creativity. To Adam, it was a very natural process and one that he held at the center of his relationship with LEGO bricks, and telling his story seemed to spark interest in those who wished to listen. Paal Smith-Meyer in particular was keen to bring Adam closer towards the LEGO Education Program because he wanted the program to build upon, adapt and begin to employ a lot of the clever reasoning and theory behind LEGO Architecture. Furthermore, Paal knew of Adam's extensive catalogue of ideas and thought that some of them could begin to surface through the LEGO Education Program. One of these particular ideas was the creation of a mechanical engineering set, which would revive the Technic simple machine sets from the 80s, but with the focus on creating mechanical devices

"It forced me, as an entrepreneur, to go about these ideas on my own"

with cutaway sections, so you could build a machine, such as an elevator, and then use the model as a tool to see and learn how it works.

With Adam solidifying an internal reputation of a maverick with great ideas, but one who is too radical and quick thinking to fit into the corporate structure, there was the growing sense that there existed this crazy asset to The LEGO Group and someone needed to find a function for him. This was when the President of LEGO Education, Harvey Dean invited Adam to have the honor of being the keynote speaker at the LEGO Education summit. The headquarters of the summit were coincidentally in Kansas City, near where Adam attended college and later lived and practiced as an architect. Adammay not have been aware of the LEGO Education Program, but he was more than willing to take up the offer and share his view on LEGO fostering education through creativity.

"When LEGO Education invited me to be their keynote speaker, at the time it was just another feather in the cap as an LCP," says Adam. With keen interest to keep his reputation alive within the corporate community, Adam accepted and in July 2012 gave a presentation on how the brick fosters education through creativity to 150 professionals within the community.

The words and actions of Adam stoked the interest of the attending visitors, and the seminar proved to be a huge success. More so was the interest in Adam as a fascinating character with a unique talent, but still the audience was left to ponder over the use and application of his talents. There were attempts to channel his thinking and even attempts to put him back into the corporate structure. None however were successful, because although ideas started off as invigorating, constant barriers to let Adam create freely meant that in the end the ideas died by the wayside. The presentation left such a lasting presence that Adam was invited over to Billund to deliver a similar presentation to The LEGO Group designers. A similar wave of uncertainty crossed their minds as the designers were stuck between whether to view Adam as delusional and wacky or a brilliant genius. This confusion of what to do with Adam made the artist come to a standstill and review his relationship with the toy giant. Was he really getting the most out of the relationship by standing by and pitching them ideas, or should he be going out on his own and making his ideas happen?

"It forced me, as an entrepreneur, to go about these ideas on my own, the roller coaster, Brickworld, the museum gallery etc." As a result, Adam began to hold ideas closer to his chest, and went back being a LCP with the intention of creating more independent projects that were detached from The LEGO Group.

The LEGO Group, however, had other ideas. With a keen interest to re-engage him into the business, Adam was bought back on board to create the architecture subsection of the Master Builder Academy, a subscription set that specialized in different themes and promised to take your building to the next level.

WHAT IS LEGO EDUCATION SERIOUS PLAY

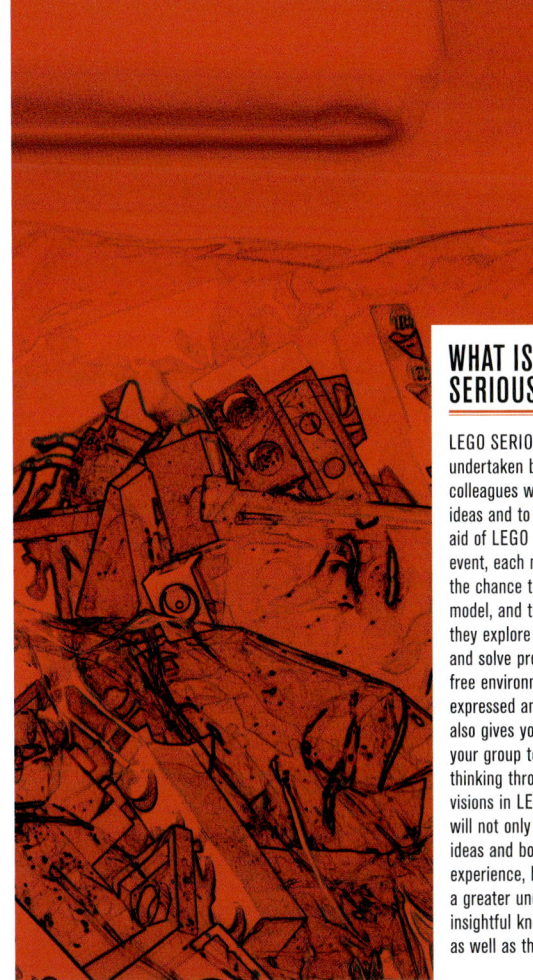

LEGO SERIOUS PLAY is an activity undertaken by businesses in which colleagues work together to communicate ideas and to solve problems with the aid of LEGO bricks. In a SERIOUS PLAY event, each member of the team will have the chance to build their own 3D LEGO model, and then listen to each other as they explore the nature of their business and solve problems in a structured but free environment. Any ideas can be expressed and listened to. SERIOUS PLAY also gives you the opportunity to open up your group to innovative and imaginative thinking through building their future visions in LEGO form. All the participants will not only leave having challenged ideas and bonded over a group building experience, but everyone leaves with a greater understanding and more insightful knowledge of their colleagues as well as themselves.

MASTER BUILDER
THE ACADEMY

A new way to explore architecture shared Adam's genius and offered LEGO fans a more knowledgeable experience, but the fantastic project came to a sudden and abrupt end

Building LEGO sets inadvertently teaches you tricks and tips that you can use to become a better builder. But in 2011, The LEGO Group released a set where the builder's gratification not only came from the building of a model, but from a series of techniques as well as inspiration from prominent builders, designers and LCP's in the LEGO community. In 2012 Adam found himself on the judging panel for the LEGOLAND Master Builder competition, which brought him closer with aspirational builders and opened up the opportunity to be a featured artist in the Master Builder Academy collection. As a full supporter of the academy, Adam was more than happy to oblige the organization.

"The idea behind it was amazing. The LEGO Group spared no expense, it was gorgeous...it just didn't really take off," explains Adam. They reached out to him as the face of LEGO Architecture to create Level Four in the series (see page 95). Adam began planning the different ways that Master Builder Academy could explore Architecture. It is always a pleasure to see brilliant concept ideas in their

BRICKS 91

MASTER BUILDER ACADEMY

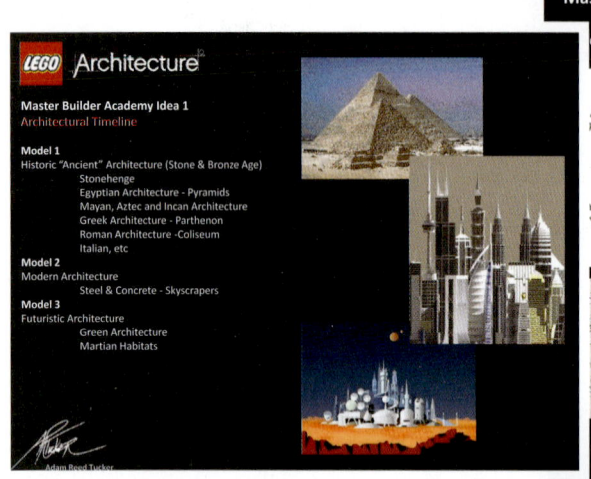

Never-before-seen slides from Adam's initial Master Builder Academy ideas presentation.

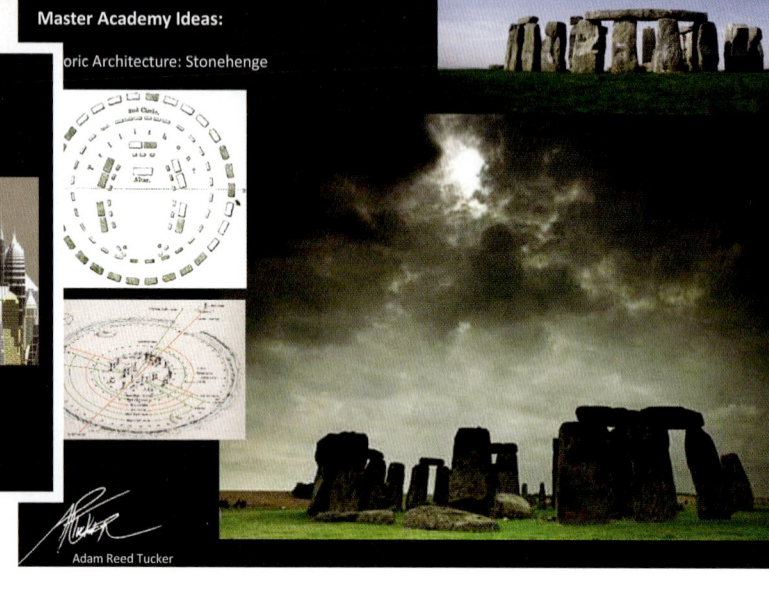

A Word from the Artist

As an Architectural Artist, Adam Reed Tucker's desire is to capture the essence of architectural structures into their pure sculptural form. First and foremost he does not view my models as literal replicas, but rather his own artistic interpretations through the use of LEGO® bricks as a design medium. The LEGO brick is not initially thought of as a material typically used in creating art or used as an artist's medium. Mr. Tucker discovered the LEGO brick was lending itself so naturally to his applications as does paint to a painter or metal to a blacksmith. As he continues to explore capturing architecture with only basic bricks, plates and tiles, he finds the challenges and possibilities they offer almost magical.

Adam Reed Tucker – Architectural LEGO® Artist, Concept Designer & Creative Developer

Building Scale

The LEGO Brick lends itself so well if you are looking to build big or small. Here I have created the Museum of Science & Industry (located in Chicago) in 2 different sizes or what architects often refer to as building scales. The larger model (1) used over 30,000 pieces, but was also created with as little of only 300 pieces (2). So no matter the size of your collection you can always build to a scale.

When building in different scales the size of your model may require you to think more creatively to solve unique problems that may present themselves. For instance, to recreate the main entry columns in the small model I used 1x2 plates with handles, when turned sideways they change to take on the shape of a column. To do this I employed a technique using sideways construction. To accomplish this there are many useful elements that can be used to change the orientation (direction) of how your constructing.

"The LEGO Group spared no expense, it was gorgeous...it just didn't really take off"

preliminary form, however when you view Adam's ideas for Level 4 Invention Designer, it leaves you in awe as every idea is simply magnificent and would have been a fantastic set. Ideas had been crafted from exploring architecture through the ages, different stages of the architectural process, blending architecture into different kinds of landscapes and even different architectural forms. Every one of these ideas could have been a different level of the Master Builder Academy, and combined with Adam's contribution of how to use techniques, to mix shapes, use colors and create different textures, they really would have made spectacular additions to The LEGO Group's portfolio.

Their value also lay in how they would emphasize the educational aspect of the Master Builder Academy. The knowledge Adam parted with included detailed information about his artistic process, as well as careful instructions about the application of his favorite techniques and also lots of information about architectural theory. It's information that is unique to Adam as both an architect and an artist.

Rather than dedicating a whole set just to architecture, The LEGO Group decided to dedicate a portion of the 2014 20215 Invention Designer to World Architecture, and much of Adam's process and techniques were shared in this section of the set. That was the last big set in the series of Master

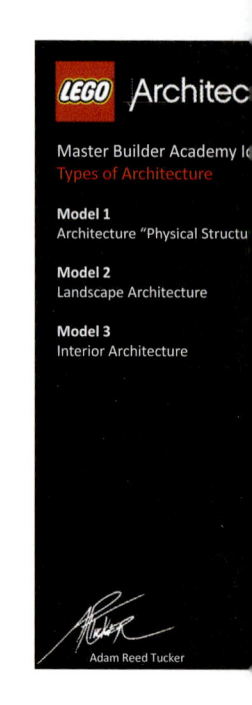

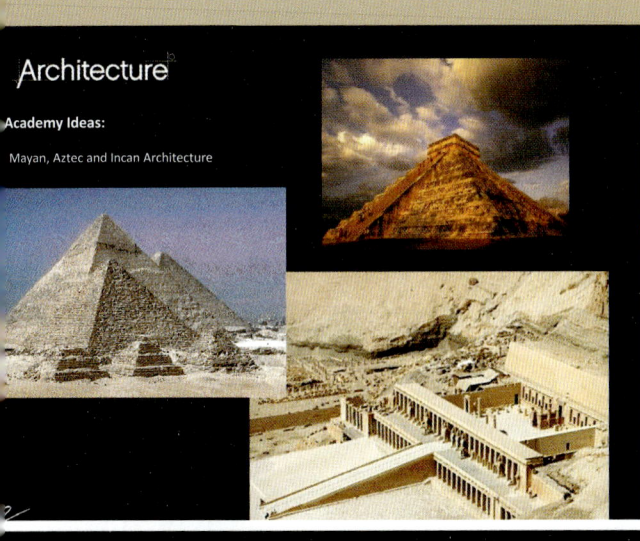

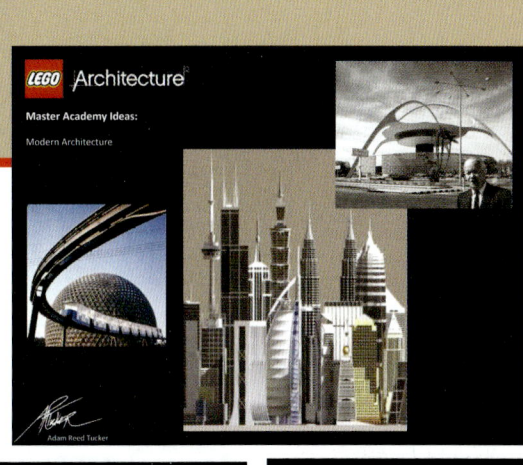

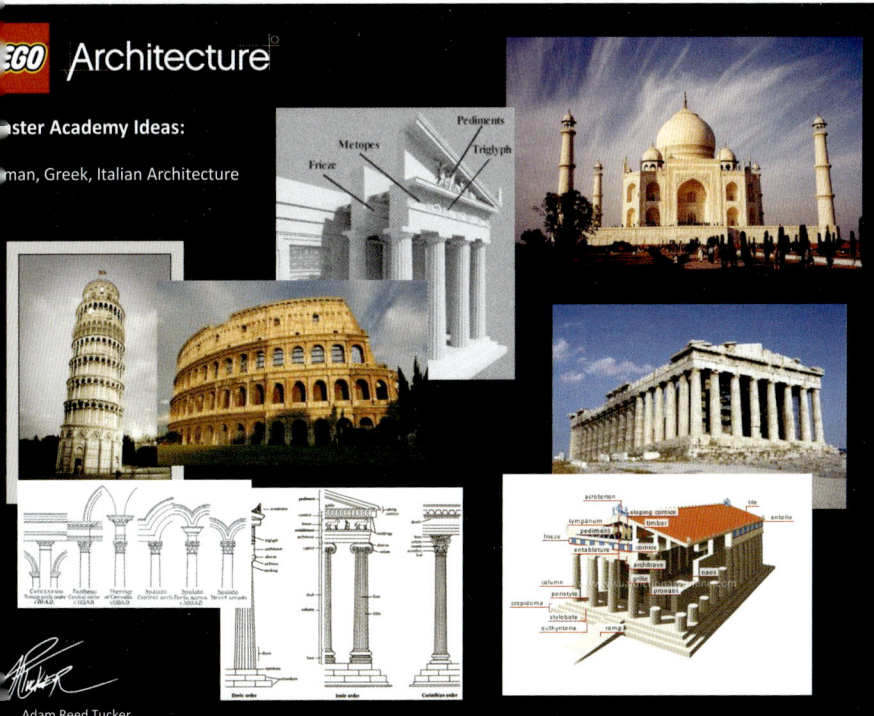

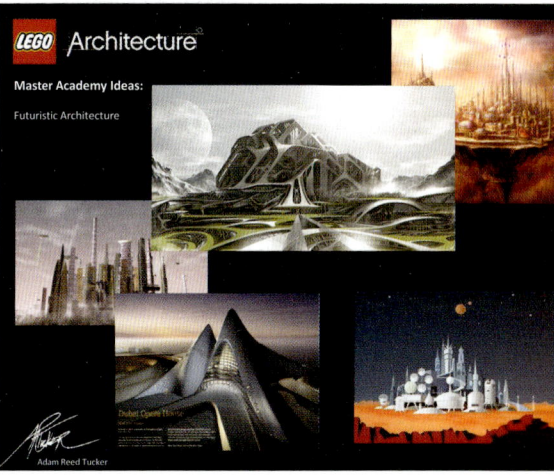

These slides suggest how Adam saw the Master Builder Academy as an opportunity to explore the story and development of Architecture through LEGO bricks.

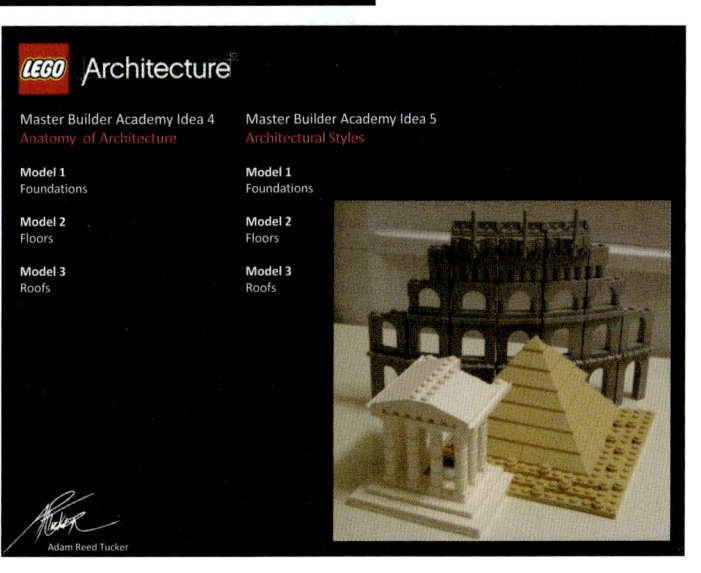

Examples of building a space ship in the first level of the Master Builder Academy: 20200 Space Designer.

"The theme came to a sudden and premature end"

Builder Academy as the theme came to a sudden and premature end, which was highly unfortunate.

There was certainly the potential to explore the theme further than a single set, and we can only speculate that it would have provided a truly unique experience. It's even suggested on the Brickset database that 20210 World Architecture was planned for release, but never came to fruition. Perhaps it was its capacity for expansion, which meant it was not suitable for publishing, but unfortunately we are only left to speculate on what it could have been. The final product, due for release in 2014, only made it to American territories and 20210, and a lot of Adam's ideas, were left in the dark. For those who don't have a copy of Level 4 20215 Invention Designer, all we are left with is the never-before-seen presentation that showcases some of the set's initial concepts, and a double-page spread that demonstrates some of the knowledge and ideas which Adam passed on.

Forever looking to the future, Adam carried on exploring fresh ideas, organizing exhibits, and creating LCP commissioned work. As for Master Builder Academy, it was left to retire to the annals and archives of retired LEGO themes.

The Master Builder Academy packaging was visually striking with it's use of color to indicate levels, and later bringing three stages together to provide a whole level in one set.

HOW MASTER BUILDER ACADEMY WORKS

Level 1
20200 Space Designer
20201 Microbuild Designer
20202 Robot Designer

Level 2
20203 Flight Designer
20204 Creature Designer
20205 Auto Designer

Level 3
20206 The Lost Village
20207 The Forbidden Bridge
20208 The Dark Lair

Level 4
20209 Time Machine
20210 World Architecture
20211 Inventor's Lab

Adam's contribution towards LEGO Master Builder Academy featured towards the end of the short-lived theme. It provided a different function to a traditional LEGO sets and was unique due to its subscription option. The premise of LEGO Master Builder Academy was to give younger builders a graded-style theme, similar to a martial art, where they could work their way through different levels to improve their building skills and technique. Each set was beautifully crafted with gorgeously detailed instruction books that taught you how to make three different kinds of models using the same bricks. Unlike creator 3-in-1 sets, it also explained and gave demonstrations of new and existing techniques by LEGO designers, LCP's and master builders. Unfortunately it was only tried and tested in America, and commands a high price on the secondary market for anyone looking to add these sets to their collection.

A sample spread from Adam's section of 20215 Invention Designer.

THE WORK OF ADAM REED TUCKER

Over the years Adam's talents have been commissioned by customers from around the globe, here are some examples of the projects he has worked on...

A close-up of Ford Field commission by Detroit Lions NFL.

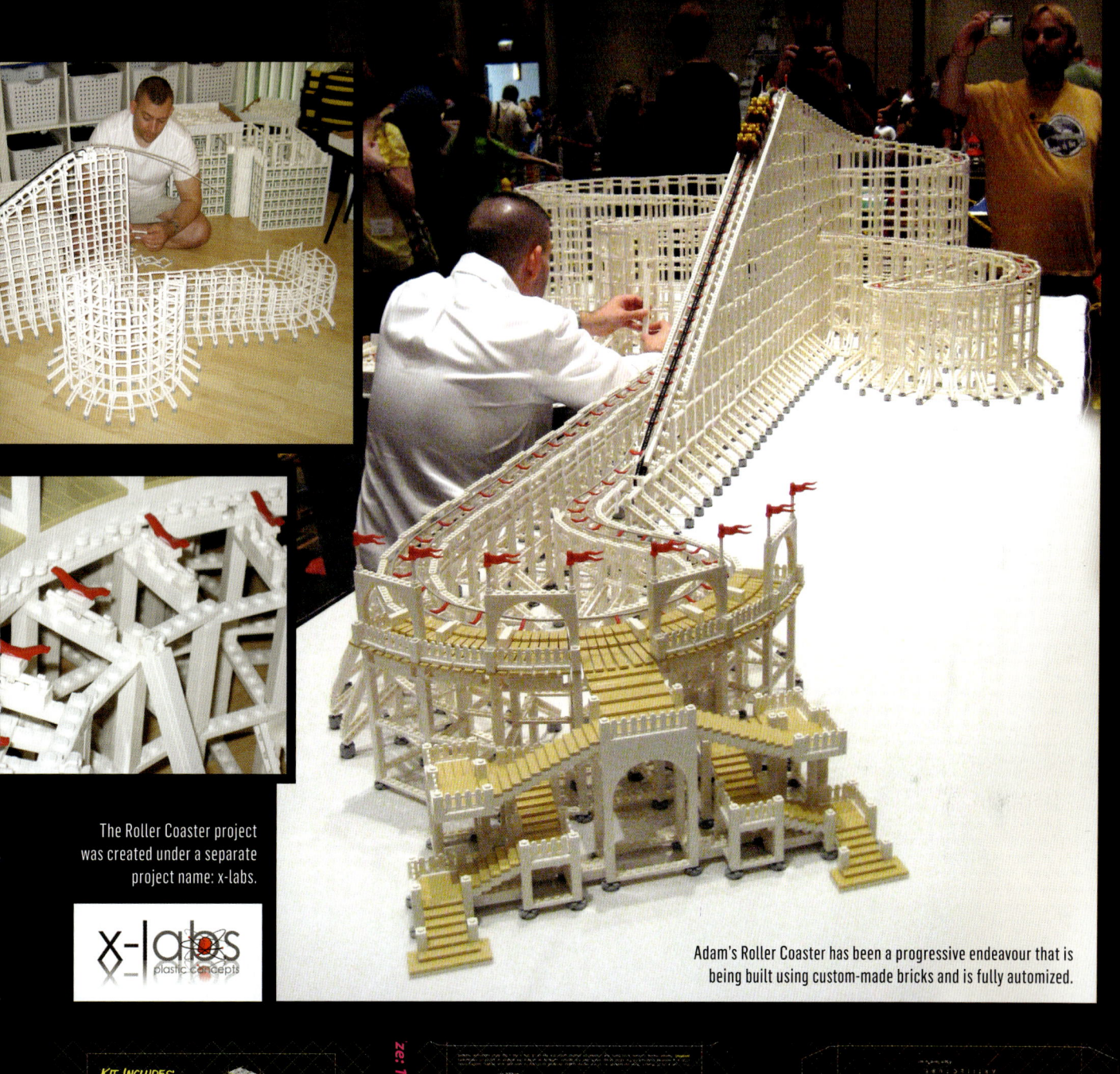

The Roller Coaster project was created under a separate project name: x-labs.

x-labs
plastic concepts

Adam's Roller Coaster has been a progressive endeavour that is being built using custom-made bricks and is fully automized.

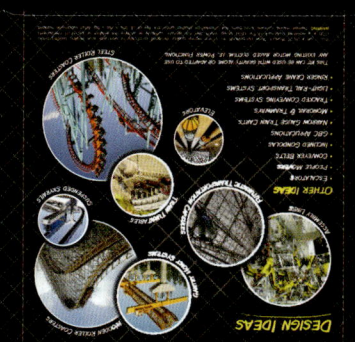

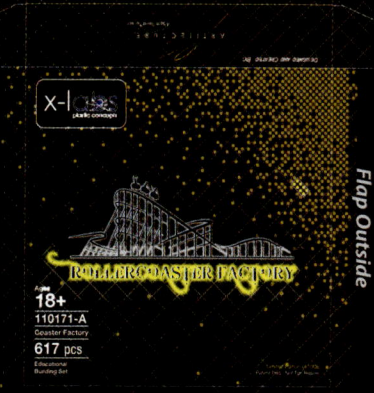

Sample artwork from the Roller Coaster set packaging, designed by Adam.

Laurie Children's Hospital, Chicago.

High Roller Observation Wheel at the Linq, Caesars Palace, Las Vegas.

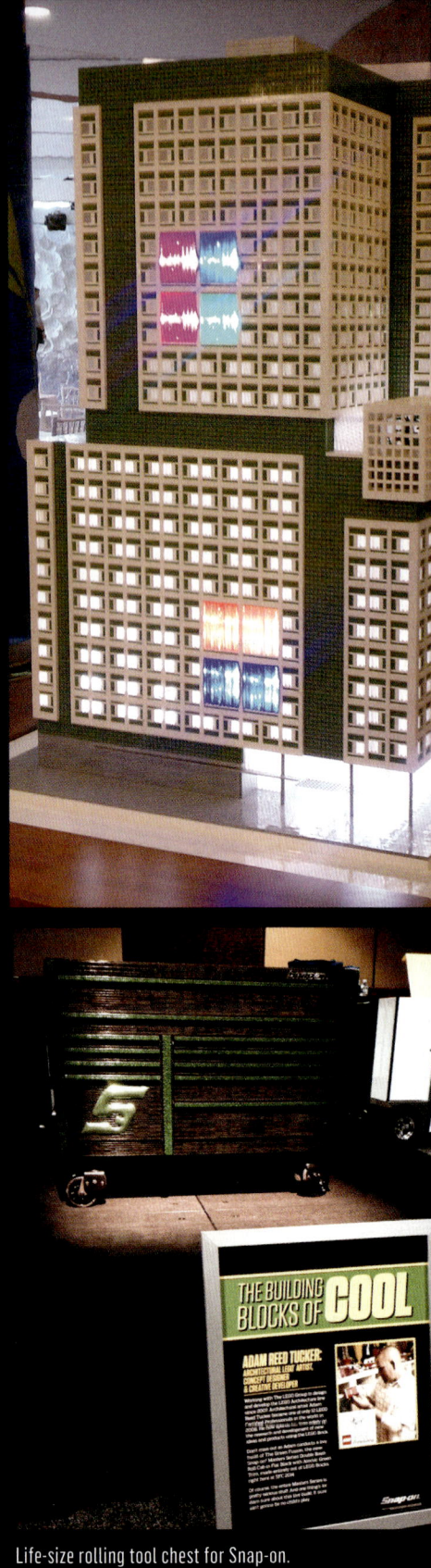

Life-size rolling tool chest for Snap-on.

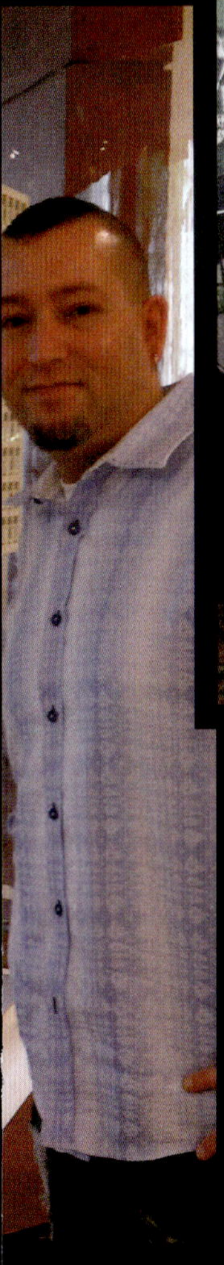

Site plan of Grand Geneva Country Club.

A commission for a private residence, Northern suburbs Chicago.

Lots of planning, hours and bricks go into every build.

Taileson West, Frank Lloyd Wright, Scottsdale, Arizona.

Jaxson, Adam's son lends a hand during construction.

Adam enjoying his visit to the studio of Frank Lloyd Wright, one of his inspirational icons.

On display at the Bank of America conference.

Adam assembles his Cinderella castle.

Adam's work is always a family affair as Jaxson offers a supporting hand during installation.

Adam with Adrian Smith & Bill Curtis.

BRICKSCULTURE 101

A VISUAL GUIDE

DK Books publishes a high-end hardback publication to showcase and immortalize the beauty of the Architecture theme. Find out why it was a natural next step and what makes it so special

The success of the LEGO Architecture range is undeniable. It is a controversial theme that tends to divide opinion, however even the most seasoned fan cannot argue that it's a range which has enriched The LEGO Group's portfolio and diversified its demographic. LEGO themes come and go, but thanks to Adam's creative approaches and unique ideas, it will be a theme that will no doubt stay with us for years to come. It comes as no surprise that The LEGO Group would want to celebrate this theme with a polished, high-quality hardback book that would showcase all the sets and celebrate their artistic vision. The book was produced by Dorling Kindersly (DK), but they worked closely with The LEGO Group to make sure that the product was presented on brand. The product was released in 2014 under the title of 'LEGO Architecture: The Visual Guide'.

It is not the first time a LEGO theme has been celebrated by DK, as there are numerous character encyclopedias that give detailed accounts of every minifigure, its contexts and vehicles in the theme, as well as including interviews with designers and graphic artists. As LEGO Architecture was a more developed and mature beast than other themes celebrated by DK, the decision was made to make sure the LEGO Architecture Visual Guide reflected the same grown-up attitude and experience that is demonstrated in each LEGO Architecture set. Once The LEGO Group and DK were happy with the agreement and the plan for the publication, The LEGO Group reached out to Adam to gauge his interest in contributing to the publication, given that Adam was an integral part of the inception and execution of the LEGO Architecture theme. Adam accepted the offer to participate in the project and waited for instructions on what content he was to provide.

The book talks briefly about Adam's creative childhood before looking at the models in the range.

Adam began playing with LEGO bricks as a boy, when an aunt bought him his first LEGO set.

Adam at work in his studio; he consults a reference book while working on the LEGO model of the Solomon R. Guggenheim Museum® in New York.

Thousands of LEGO bricks are stored in Adam's Chicago studio.

The 'LEGO Architecture Visual Guide' comes in a hard case, which speaks the same luxurious tone as the models in the range.

| A VISUAL GUIDE

The book not only presents the range's models in their various angles but it also pulls them apart and presents them in an exploded image so you can see the models layer by layer.

104 BRICKS CULTURE

"The key is that the model is a representation, not an exact replication"

The main process was similar to the Master Builder Academy in that The LEGO Group wanted Adam to talk about his process, but also they were keen to get Adam's narrative on the development of the models that came to be, as well as the artistic theory he puts into his work. As the book would have a very structured and ergonomic approach, the publishers decided that the best way to get Adam to express his story would be to allow him to write the foreword and then to tackle his background, process and development through a series of chapters told in the third person. Although it is somewhat cathartic to re-live his days creating LEGO Architecture sets, it did make the artist reflect on the constant limitations put in place by The LEGO Group in order to produce a model fit for sale.

"When I was asked about my process and how we chose buildings the truth is a lot of that is based on pragmatic business decisions. For example, can we get licensing? What are sales channels going to be? Are the parts that are needed in the active part element channel?"

The limitations placed on artists when they are dealing with the creative process create a shift in the way artists will express themselves. Rather than focusing on pure expression of an idea, it invigorates the artist by challenging them to work within restraints, and can be seen as an artistic interpretation of a question, the question being the brief that set the limitations.

Adam describes the process in the Visual Guide: "The key is that the model is a representation, not an exact replication." All of a sudden, the simplistic and minimalist nature of the LEGO Architecture sets becomes even more apparent, thought through and highly sophisticated. It falls into a state between realism and abstract art where the subject matter is interpreted into a new form that is recognizable but still an artistic interpretation. Looking through the guide, which takes you through each build and images of its subject matter, you gain a much higher appreciation and understanding of why LEGO Architecture sets take on their given form and the journey which was embarked on to create them.

The book is a beautiful asset to any LEGO Architecture fan, and goes a considerable way to celebrate not only the sets themselves, but also the subject matters and the people who created them. The insights from Adam and author Philip Wilkinson, will not only give anyone a further appreciation of the LEGO Architecture range and an understanding of the inner workings of a LEGO theme, but the pages that tell the story – and the images that illustrate it – are so beautifully presented in a mature and sophisticated fashion that is undeniably unique for a LEGO title. It commands a prime spot on anyone's bookshelf.

THE CRITICAL GAZE

One part of the story that the visual guide didn't explore was how the theme settled with the fans. The LEGO Architecture range may feel like it is meant to be embraced by adult fans, but it always provides an interesting topic of conversation. Generally the fan community is rather split on its value and appeal. Parts of the community love the mature and substantial building process, the genius and usage of interesting parts, working in a different scales and the reward gained from the piece of art you are left with. Others in the community lay their critical gaze over the theme and complain about its design and high price point. Whilst the price point can be seen as rather high for the bricks you buy, the same fans that complain about these models show no issue with spending the same amount of money per brick on other licensed themes, such as Star Wars. It's interesting that some are willing to overlook one theme but criticize another for the same reason, however success is often governed by the adverse reaction to the art, and surrealist artist Salvador Dali would even go so far as to say that a successful reaction from an audience makes a piece of art "less exciting".

Whilst there will always be those who judge, those few may not take into consideration the restraints placed on the artist when they create. "Some people say, for example, that my Sydney Opera House looks like the Sarlacc from 'Star Wars Episode VI: Return of the Jedi'. [But regardless of whether they're right or wrong] I could only use a handful of different elements, in two different colors, with active elements, which once all added together didn't breach a certain price point… and I only had two weeks to design it," Adam recalls. "Constructive criticism is fine, but criticize in the knowledge of the building circumstances," he adds. This comment strikes to the core of the complaints, and emphasizes the artistic integrity behind each model as a representation of a subject matter. This is evident in the display and credit of the artist on each of the boxes.

It could be suggested that the re-release of certain models, such as the Burj Khalifa, fuelled this practice of slating Adam's work, however the success of the architecture line meant that over time models have been allowed more pieces per set, and as the theme has gone onto achieve success more pieces that are necessary have been created and the restrictions on colors, bricks and subject matter has changed. There is of course one definitive way to look at whether a theme is a success or a failure, and that is to look at whether or not the theme is still active, and as the LEGO Architecture range seems to show no sign of slowing down the theme can only be deemed a success.

LEGO BRICKUMENTARY

A MOMENT IN THE LIMELIGHT

By 2015 Adam's use of the LEGO brick had captured people's imaginations and he soon found himself being followed by camera crews as they documented his work for an upcoming release

In 2015 director and writer Daniel Judge released the documentary film 'A LEGO Brickumentary'. Other than the rather ill-coined title, and the fact that it was a huge commercial failure, it's a rather pleasant film that successfully explores the Brick and its culture.

"The creators of the film wanted to capture another side of the LEGO universe. They wanted a film about the Brick that would depict people of all ages and interests creatively engaging with LEGO sets," explains Adam – who was one of the people featured in the documentary. The documentary starts with the introduction of a narrator, presented in the form of a minifigure, voiced by Hollywood actor Jason Bateman. Bateman's friendly and harmless tone is perfect for the role as it seems to reflect the kind natured values of The LEGO Group, whilst also serving as a vehicle to bring familiarity and explanation to the subject matter. To further normalize the appeal of LEGO sets, the documentary features up-close and personal interviews with famous faces who enjoy building LEGO sets. The faces include: singer songwriter Ed Sheeran, who spent his first royalty check on the Death Star; creator of South Park Trey Parker who enjoys building sets after work for their therapeutic value; and professional baseball player Dwight Howard who enjoys building as a creative outlet. Whilst Judge may have splashed out to get the big names, famous LEGO faces also star in the film, including: Senior Director of The LEGO Group Tormod Askildsen, Director of the New Business Group for The LEGO Group Paal Smith-Meyer and, of course, LCP LEGO artist and founder of the LEGO Architecture range, Adam Reed Tucker.

Our minifigure narrator takes us through a stop-motion history of the LEGO brand and its origins from a small toy shop in Billund, Denmark, right up to the plastic empire that we see today. It then goes on, with an extremely fast pace, to look at the lives of many different AFOLs who enjoy LEGO bricks such as creator of the Cuusoo Mars Rover Stephen Pakbaz, Brick-film makers, Patch art work, MOCers from around the world and the story of LEGO Architecture. Adam's story features as the tale of LEGO's history reaches the release of LEGO Mindstorms, and the subsequent hacking that instigated the change in attitude that led to bringing external ideas into the group. This is when we learn about our artist's life and his determination to bring the LEGO Architecture brand to market. The film even directly attributes the success of the LEGO Architecture to the will and determination of the artist.

To visually tell the story, the crew traveled to Adam's Chicago studio and spent the day filming in his house and interviewing him. Then spent a few days in Michigan filming one of his exhibits and then back to the studio for further interviewing. The four-day process meant that a lot of footage would inevitably end up on the cutting room floor after Adam's five-minute segment was created, but such is the nature of film work. As it was Adam's first time being filmed for a documentary, the lack of control for presenting his story meant that the artist had a slight fear of being misrepresented during the intrusive and elongated experience. But as Adam recalls, it was a far easier experience than he could have imagined. "They pretty much let me be myself. There were no re-takes, forcing or faking. Nothing was staged. I just got on with what I was meant to be doing and it was all very raw, or at least my experience with it was," explains Adam.

Forever humble, even though Adam owns a copy and his picture is featured on the box, somehow the artist has just been too busy to watch the film. "I probably should see it, but then again I haven't seen the LEGO Movie either," says Adam as he smiles and thinks about all the projects that he's been busy with the past few years. Being featured in the documentary certainly paid off as the next challenge Adam would go on to face would be one of his biggest, and most financially exhausting projects to date.

THE VERDICT

A LEGO Brickumentary is a documentary that will fascinate those who aren't familiar with the extended LEGO universe. It paints a picture of the fans being people who wholeheartedly accept 'geek' culture and unashamedly embrace the love they have for the brick. Granted, the celebrity and artist appearances do help to normalize the tone, however as the film goes on you do continue to get the feeling that it is a community made up of the 'other'. It feels a little detached from the rest of the world, but perhaps that is just how the filmmakers perceived the LEGO universe.

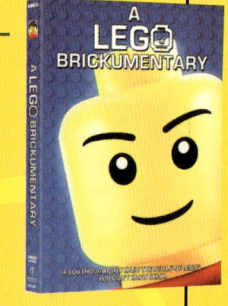

By the end of the film one thing is certain, you are sold to the idea that LEGO is a wonderful creative outlet for many people. That being said the fast pace of the film does make it feel like the running time is a little long, and perhaps it would have engaged its audience more and gone on to achieve more success had it been a one-hour TV special rather than a feature film with a cinematic release. It has value, but it's not something you will be in a rush to engage with again, not like a brilliant LEGO set anyway.

A LEGO BRICKUMENTARY

IF YOU THOUGHT YOU KNEW THE WORLD OF LEGO,
YOU DON'T KNOW BRICK.

| BRICK BY BRICK

BRICK by BRICK

A joint endeavor between Adam and the Museum of Science and Industry produces a sequel exhibit that plays tribute to the engineering marvels of the world with great success

Adam's touring exhibitions had grown from a small set-up in a local discovery center to being one of the main exhibits at a national museum. Its success had not only proved useful in keeping Adam's name afloat, and maintaining a presence on the exhibition circuit, but the endeavor also provided a regular income that could support the artist whilst he embarked on other creative ventures. After a successful first exhibition, the Museum of Science and Industry, Chicago (MSI) contacted Adam in 2012 to open up a dialogue about creating a sequel to their 2010 show Art + Science = Architecture. As the first exhibit mainly focused on models of skyscrapers, Adam was left to have a creative contemplation about how to theme the next show.

"First I coined the title Vertical Architecture, as all the pieces in the exhibition were skyscrapers. I wanted to be a little whimsical, and a little Willy Wonka, and go from vertical architecture to horizontal engineering.

BRICK by BRICK

BRICK by BRICK
LEGO
Certified Professional
Adam Reed Tucker

BUILD AN ARENA THAT OUTLIVES AN EMPIRE
BRICK by BRICK
BUILD A BRIDGE THAT SUSPENDS DISBELIEF
BRICK by BRICK

| BRICK BY BRICK

For the museum's 80th anniversary, Adam built a replica of the building.

Adam, with his giant Ferris Wheel and the original source of inspiration (right).

"The exhibition would stretch...to include ancient engineering marvels... up to present-day architecture"

which to me meant bridges," recalls Adam. It was thought this approach might provide enough continuity between the two exhibits to re-engage the audience, attract new members to the museum and also give Adam fresh stimuli to create from. It would provide a shift in focus and architectural theory as when building skyscrapers you focus around compression, whereas with bridges the focus is on tension.

In 2014, MSI began planning the exhibit with Adam. While the exhibit's team thought bridges are a compelling form of architecture to display, it was decided that it could be too restrictive of a topic. Instead, the two parties further explored horizontal engineering, leading to the discussion of modern marvels around the world. This allowed for open interpretation of the theme and could still include bridges, but the subjects that make up the exhibition would stretch across a timeline to include ancient engineering marvels, such as the Roman Colosseum, right up to present-day architecture such as One World Trade Center.

Each party gave themselves time to reflect on what buildings they deemed to be important when considering engineering marvels of the world. The Museum of Science and Industry came back with their structure choices, as did Adam. It was important for Adam to build structures he felt would represent his specific aesthetic. As a result Adam had chosen his candidates by not just looking at their current significance but their geometrical, geographical and historical appeal as well as their popularity. These values weren't the only ones to be considered; Adam wanted to make sure that his take on the structures could be fresh, unique and memorable.

The exhibition was renamed *Brick by Brick* and, with contracts in place and an exhibition to create, on January 1, 2015 Adam took to his home studio to create the selected engineering marvels. A year on, or more precisely 3,200 hours of work later, Adam emerged with 12 new LEGO structures. To put into perspective how much effort that process took, the average American will work 2,000 hours a year. The creation process for the models was nothing short of complex. Each of the 12 models would not only have to be researched, designed and then built but they all had to be modular and fit for transportation.

"How do you move a 60-foot-long Golden Gate Bridge? How do you move a 12-foot roller coaster that requires precise and a fragile latticework to operate it? There are just so many factors you need to incorporate," explains Adam. Over the course of 3,200 hours, Adam would spend roughly 1,200 hours planning and researching his subject, 800 hours designing and 1,200 hours building. But the hard work was far from complete.

Once the 12 models were finished they would need to be disassembled into their modular counterparts and then packed into trucks ready for the journey

A look into the build process of the Ferris Wheel model.

| BRICK BY BRICK

"My existing traveling exhibit takes me six hours to set up, this one takes more than two weeks"

from Adam's home studio to the Museum of Science and Industry. It would be an arduous voyage that would take, if all went to plan, around 10 days. Once all the models arrived at the museum, the work began to re-assemble his structures and, in some cases, fix his precious creations. Just like his touring exhibition, a major problem with installing *Brick by Brick* is that as Adam created the sculptures on his own he was the only person who can assemble them. One by one Adam unloaded the crates and began to rebuild. Each model took between two and 12 hours to set up, but some would inevitably need more time than others. The Golden Gate Bridge set the record for taking the longest time to construct at more than two days to unbox and set up ready for display. Adam's demand for a high level of authenticity meant that the 60-foot cabling for the bridge had to be hand-threaded on site. It's a long process and one that would largely go completely unnoticed, but the unknown efforts of the artist can be realized by those who truly see the art. Altogether, the unloading and assembly of the entire exhibition took 14 days to complete but Adam hopes it will stay there for a long time to come.

"My hope, if this exhibit travels, is that it will remain at each location for extended periods. My existing traveling exhibit takes me six hours to set up, this one takes over two weeks," he adds. Such is the level of detail and quality of *Brick by Brick*.

To accompany the LEGO sculptures, and to channel the onset inspiration at the source, the exhibition features interactive zones which take the freshly inspired visitors and give them a creative challenge to undertake. These stages include a LEGO build area where you construct a model and then test it against seismic conditions by placing it on an earthquake table and wind loading by testing it in a wind tunnel. There aren't only LEGO-inspired tasks at hand, visitors are invited to work out the best way to fold paper to create a strong bridge and test it by putting a series of weights on it, as well as an interactive simple machine station where guests can lift themselves or a friend. All the interactive stages tie in with the theme of engineering marvels of the world, and aid in making *Brick by Brick* an exhibition that will resonate in the visitor's mind the way childhood visits to the Museum of Science and Industry resonated through Adam's. The efforts and strife that Adam endured to create *Brick by Brick* may have tested the artist's endurance and creativity to the bone, but the resulting art holds value far beyond the toil of time.

Adam's monumental SNOT Golden Gate Bridge is over 60-feet long.

| BRICK BY BRICK

EXHIBIT FEATURES

The majority of the models in the exhibit are created with a minimalist approach. The inspiration from idols such as Walt Disney mean that each model captures the essence of its subject matter. Each sculpture tells a story that can be interpreted through its design. These stories make the models unique to the artist, providing depth and logic to their form.

ELEMENT PANELS

An interesting element of *Brick by Brick* is that every display comes complete with a 48x48 baseplate that depicts the elements used to create that particular structure. The 48x48 is there to demonstrate that these Goliath structures are created using a minimal amount of simple bricks that you more than likely have in your own brickventory. Despite the thousands of different elements LEGO has produced, there are only around 150 different elements in six different colors that make up the *Brick by Brick* exhibition, proving you too can create something magnificent with simple bricks at home.

114 BRICKS CULTURE

The Gateway Arch in St. Louis, Missouri manifested in the brick.

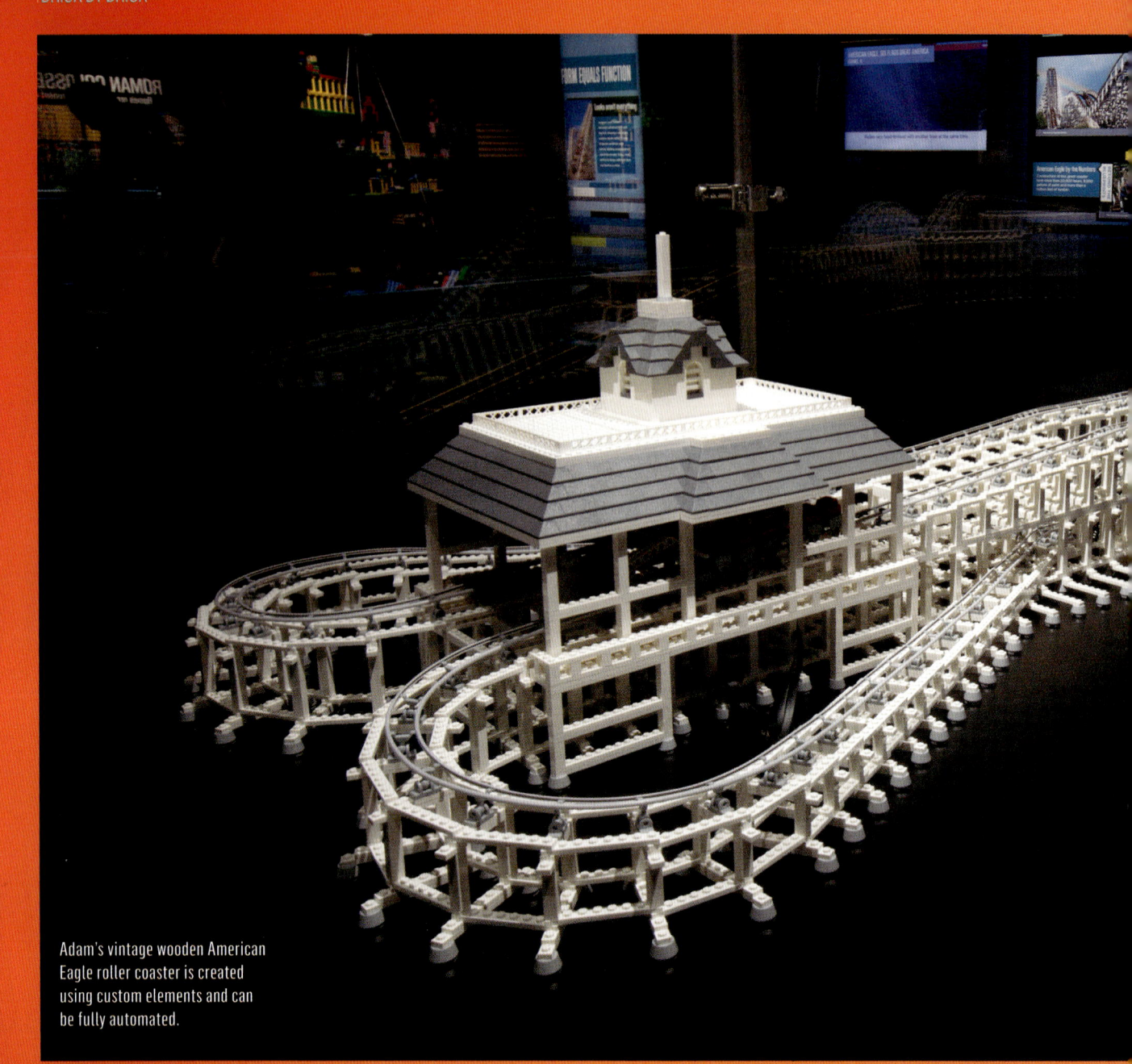

BRICK BY BRICK

Adam's vintage wooden American Eagle roller coaster is created using custom elements and can be fully automated.

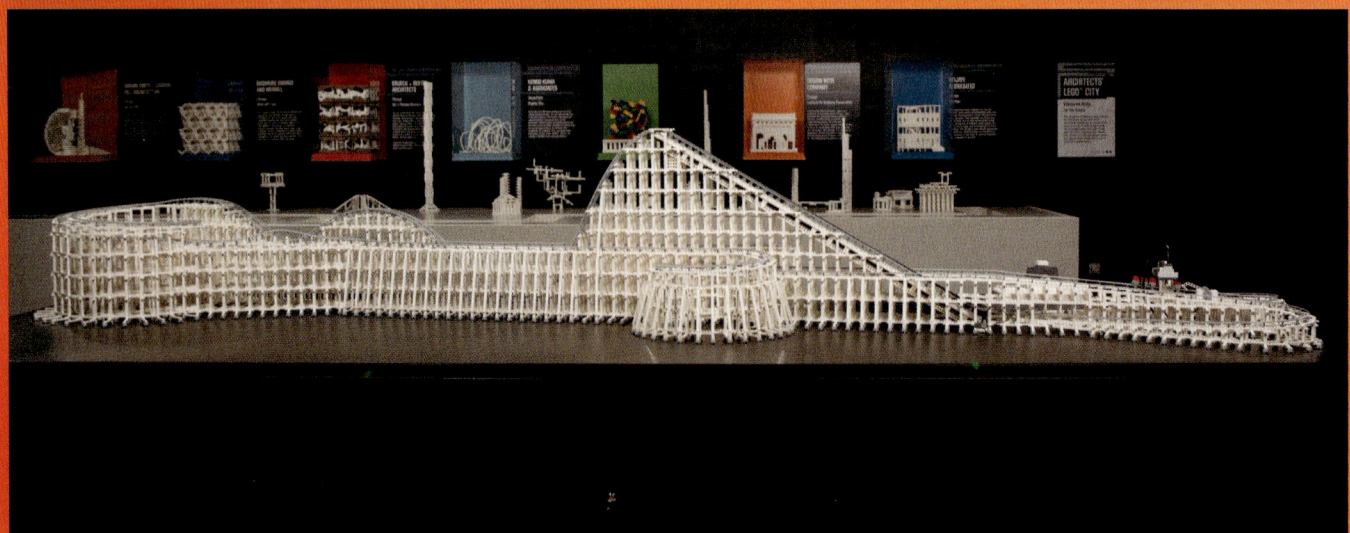

116 BRICKS CULTURE

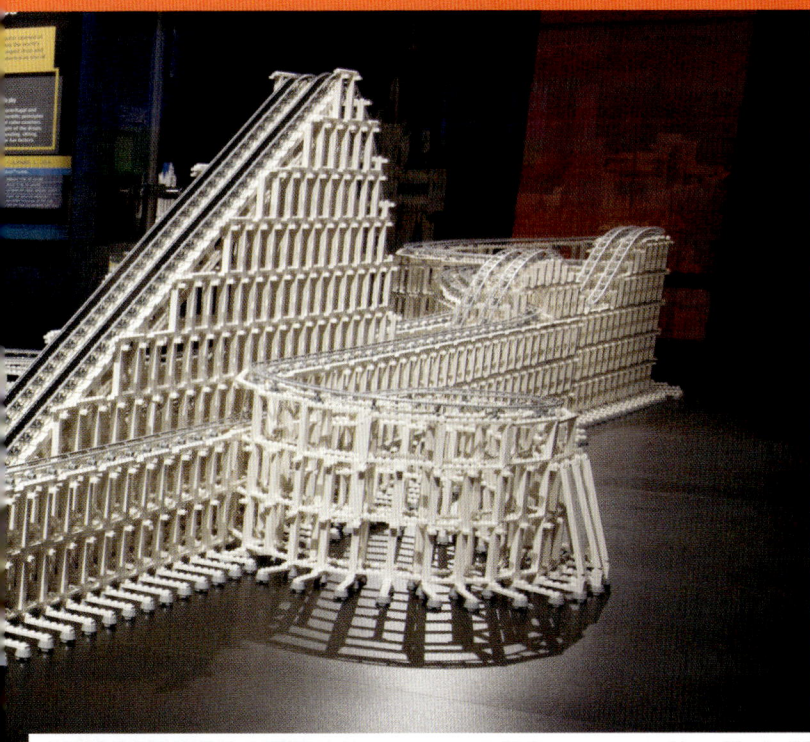

AMERICAN EAGLE ROLLER COASTER

Like the Hoover Dam, the American Eagle roller coaster is a stark contrast to the other sculptures in the exhibition. Whilst sculptures such as the Burj Khalifa and Cinderella's Castle boast an array of unnecessary aesthetically pleasing devices, the vintage wooden roller coaster is built so its form follows its function. There is nothing to create a visual aesthetic or a sense of emotion. You could argue that its height evokes emotion, but its height is only there to provide the function of falling at speed to create a thrill. The beauty in its form is that there is nothing fancy, just a striped-back construction where every piece of wood is vitally placed to fight a force. This makes it a unique piece of architecture that is created using white bricks so its form can be admired without any restraints.

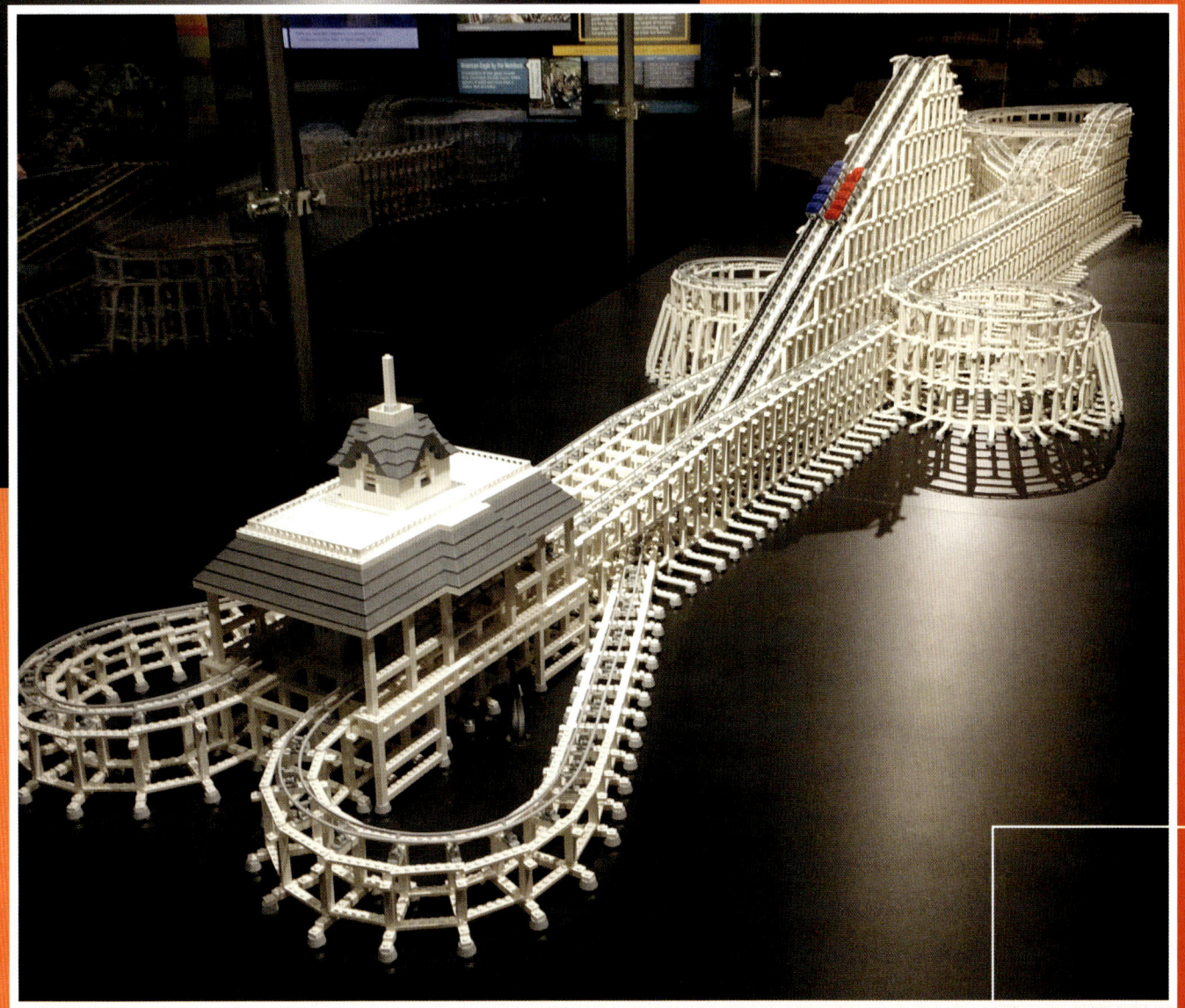

FALLINGWATER

An upscale model of Fallingwater is depicted with emphasis on how the surrounding landscape provides architectural challenges.

INTERNATIONAL SPACE STATION

Adam's International Space Station model uses more than 2,500 rare, hard-to-come-by gold 1x2 tiles for the solar panels.

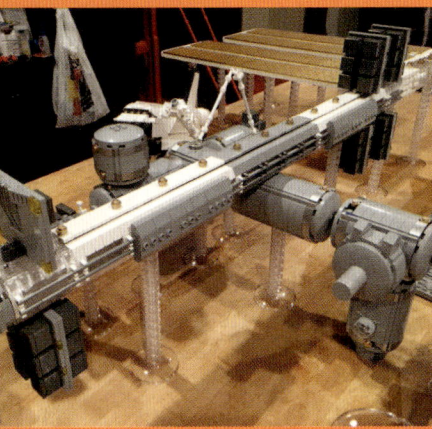

| BRICK BY BRICK

THE COLOSSEUM

This unique interpretation of the ancient Roman structure is certainly one of the most striking and visually interesting pieces in *Brick by Brick*. Originally Adam's intentions were to create a model that showed you a cross section of the Colosseum and how the walls and floors were constructed. Not satisfied that this would provide an artistic enough interpretation of the Colosseum, Adam decided that to show the inner structure of the famous Roman amphitheater he would create a static time-lapse build. To do this Adam designed the structure as a clock face, with one representing the beginning of the build and 12 representing the finished build. This creates three effects: it allows you to see piece by piece the construction of the great amphitheater; it lets you to see how Adam built the model and the techniques he employed; and finally, when viewed from above, it creates the optical illusion that the building is being erected and deteriorating to rubble. It is a brilliant representation of the historical amphitheater, as well as the effect time and withering has on ancient structures.

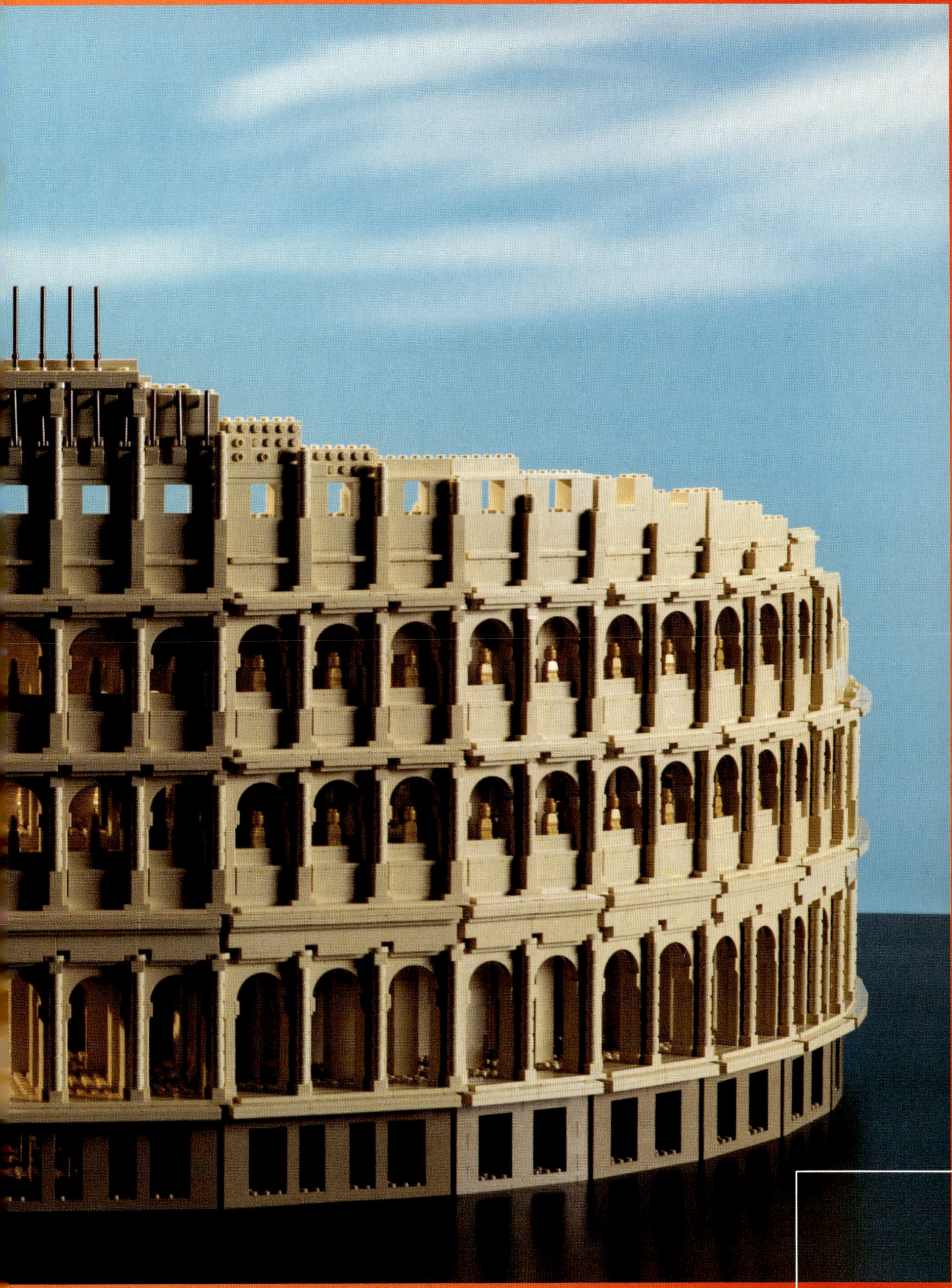

BRICK BY BRICK

"It creates the optical illusion that the building is being erected and deteriorating"

Visitors get an understanding of how the Colosseum is constructed in real life as well as the LEGO techniques Adam used to create it.

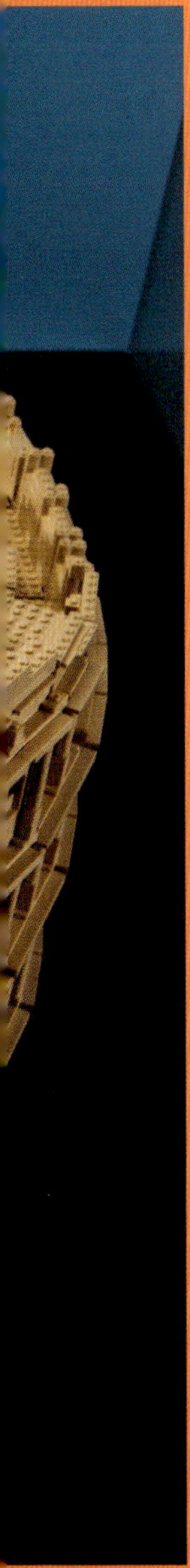

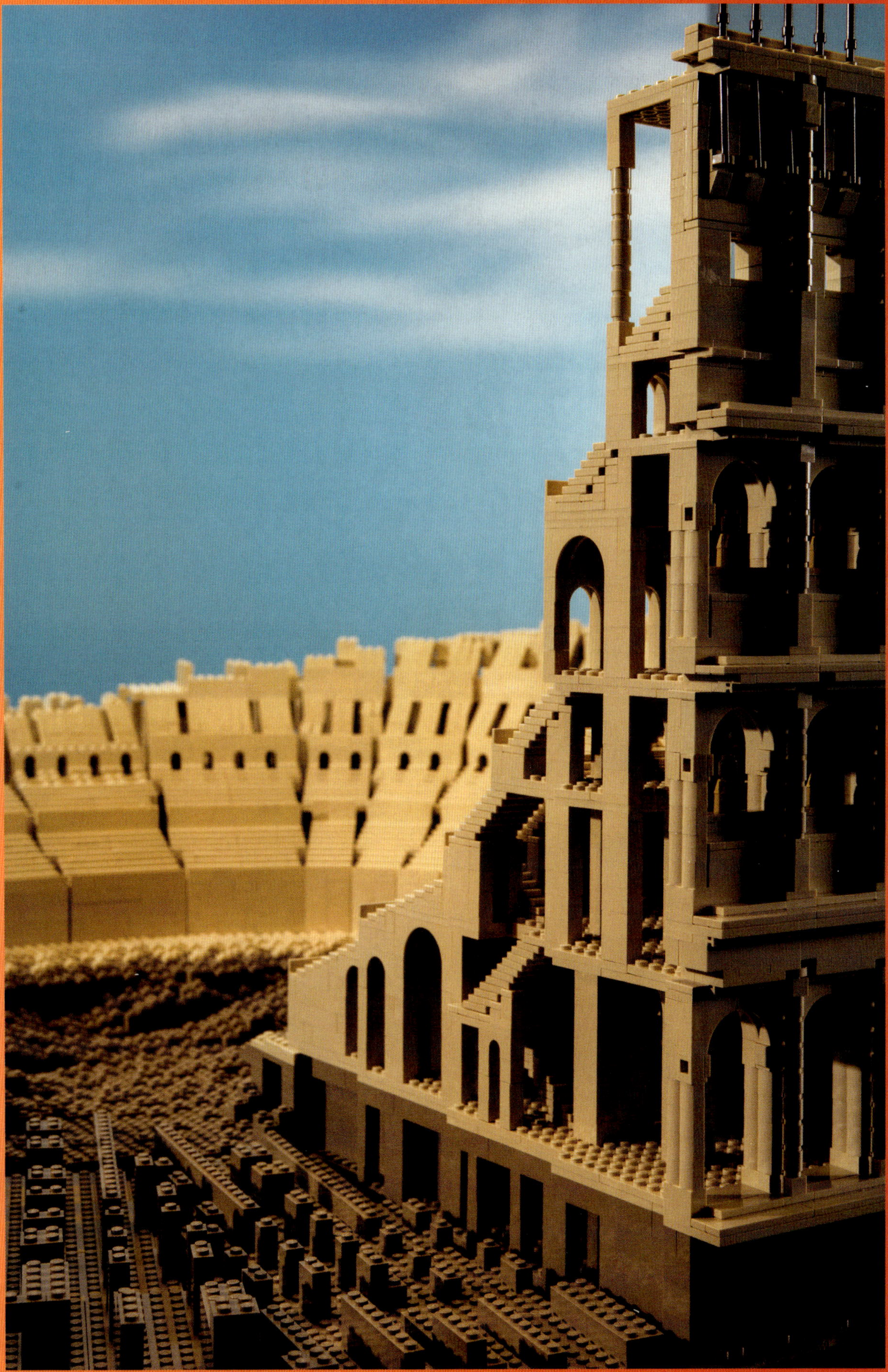

BRICK BY BRICK

Hoover Dam is built in grayscale rather than monochrome to reflect how it's depicted in black and white pictures.

HOOVER DAM

When juxtaposed with the vibrant Golden Gate Bridge and Cinderella's Castle, which light up the exhibit, the grayscale Hoover Dam can seem a little uninspiring at first but it's actually a genius creation. The thoughts behind the color choice come from a subtle epiphany during the research process. While we may take it for granted today, color photography only became common in the 1960s, and affordable and reliable enough for general household use in the 1970s. Having been built between 1931 and 1936, the Hoover Dam's construction and launch was documented using black & white photography and film. To pay homage to this, the whole build is created in grayscale, using light grey, dark grey, black, white, and clear bricks to represent the water.

BRICKS CULTURE 125

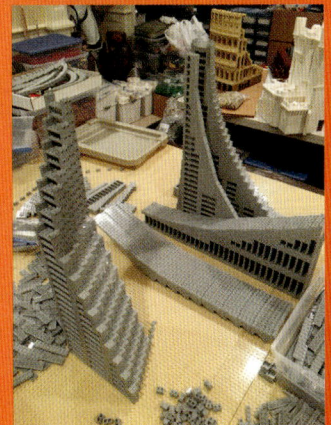

|BRICK BY BRICK

DISNEY CASTLE
A colossal Disney Castle is Adam's homage to one of his biggest influences, Walt Disney.

BRICKSCULTURE 127

BRICK BY BRICK

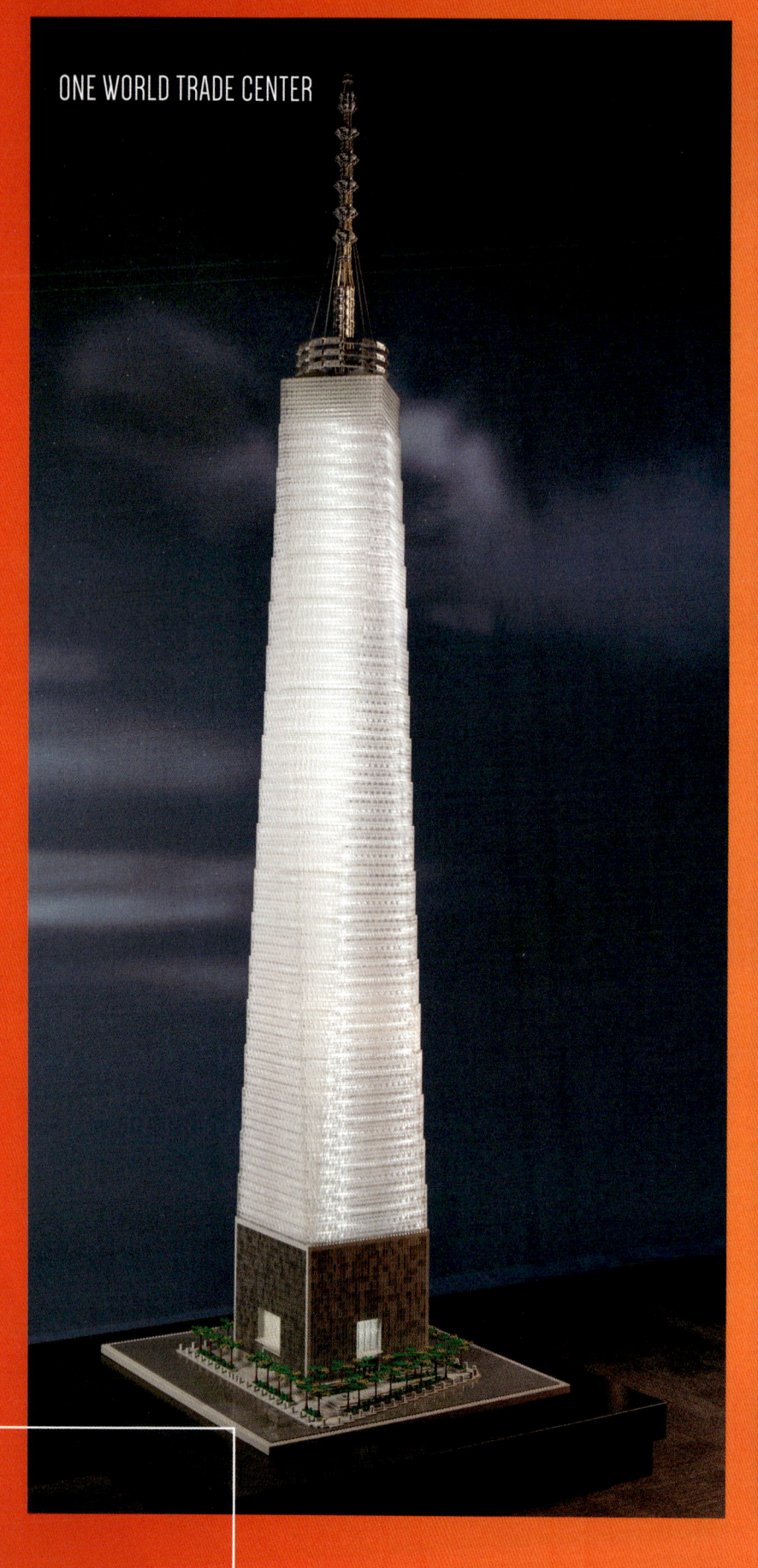

ONE WORLD TRADE CENTER

BURJ KHALIFA

PING AN FINANCE CENTER IN SHANGHAI

Although it stands as an impressive representation of the Shanghai structure, the Ping An Finance Center is actually designed to show the anatomy of the construction process. When observing the sculpture you can see how the structure is made up of a concrete and steel framework, as well as where the cladding and skinning of the building is formed. The foundation work and caseins are also exposed, as well as the route that makes up the elevator shafts. All these elements allow the viewer an almost X-ray-like view of the structure and offer an idea of how it was constructed.

BRICKS CULTURE 129

BRICK BY BRICK

130 BRICKSCULTURE

GOLDEN GATE BRIDGE

There have been many LEGO versions of the Golden Gate Bridge, yet none quite match the scale of Adam's 60-foot-long creation. Adam's sculpture is also unique for its dedication to representing the story of the subject matter. The Golden Gate Bridge was opened in 1937 and was constructed using more than 1,200,000 rivets, all applied by hand. Inspired by this fact, and in an attempt to give his bridge some texture, Adam built the whole bridge and its towers using the Studs Not On Top (SNOT) technique to represent these rivets. Consequently, the whole model had to be constructed on its side in order to change the angle of the studs. The studs are obviously not to the scale of the actual rivets, but when you look at the bridge from afar they do give the impression of texture and provides another insight into the construction methods used to created the modern marvel.

|BRICK BY BRICK

The model shows how we believe the pyramids were constructed and the chambers within.

PYRAMIDS

Adam decided to tell the story of how we believe the pyramids were built and what the internal bowels look like. As a result, the models appear to be solid structures until you venture around them to examine the cross section, revealing the King and Queen's chambers, grand gallery and the airshafts. This also gave a good opportunity to show how they were constructed and, as a result, the core, stonework and skinning are all done in different colors and textures to highlight their locations. This removes the common misconception that they are just a pile of stacked stone blocks, and enriches the viewer's knowledge of the great Egyptian pyramids.

"I wanted to be a little whimsical, and a little Willy Wonka"

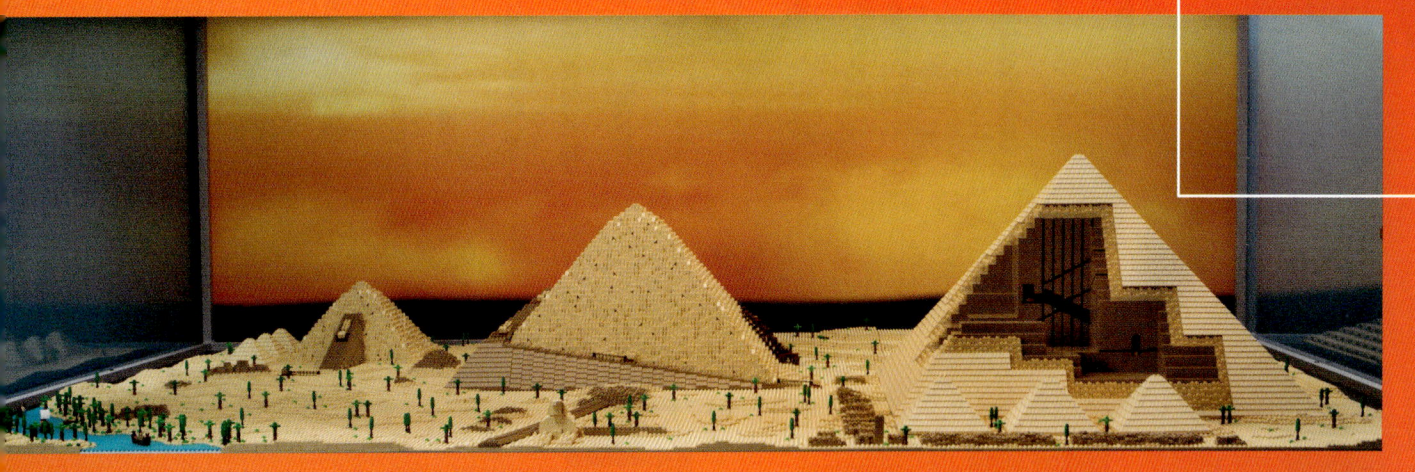

CONSIDERING THE CLASSICS

Adam is more than a LEGO artist: he is a fan at heart and looks back at some of those official sets that hold a special place within his LEGO journey

Even after a life immersed in building and engaging with bricks, every seasoned LEGO fan will have their favorites. It could be the set that got you engaged for the first time as a child, the set you shared with your siblings, the set that brought you back as an adult, or the set you have always wanted and finally purchased. We all have them. For Adam, even though he has a vast collection that spans from LEGO's conception to the modern day, it's still the classic sets of his childhood and early adult life that remain his faithful favorites. Here, Adam takes us through the sets that stole his heart and helped shape his appreciation and understanding for LEGO construction.

"The original Classic Space Line is still to this day by far and above my favorite LEGO Line ever. The reason for this is simple: strong originality. A minimal and complementary use of color allows for a diverse element pallet which naturally lends itself to fantastic, yet believable play experiences. Finally, this balanced combination creates perfect escapism, which engages and captivates both children and adults alike.

"These three castles (right) are a wonderful example of evolutionary development by The Lego Group, and yet they remain individualistic and true to the spectrums of medieval castle representation.

"What I enjoyed most about the Pirate line can be expressed through these three ships. All of them are clear representations of pirate ships and yet each are formed using unique size, color, style and complexities that not only complement but distinguish one from another.

"LEGO 855 [Mobile Crane] was my first exploration with the advanced 'system' line, otherwise known as Expert Builder, today known as LEGO Technic. The ability to graduate from

BRICKSCULTURE 135

static role play to kinetic mechanical function provided a logical way for my engagement with the brick to progress. For their time, these two sets were the single best representations of the abilities possible with the brick and aided my development and interest in mechanical knowledge.

"Trains provided a unique opportunity for LEGO fans. For the first time you could really make your system brick come to life, an action that before was only available with imagination. Again, these sets captured my attention because their color scheme, design and function portrayed reality.

"Fort Legorado was a favorite of mine, too, as it brought me back to a time when I was younger playing with Playmobil, they had a western set I absolutely loved. The Mainstreet set was a neat departure from other town sets as you had the very first tower crane where you not only prebuilt the section or wall panels but then were able to erect them just like a real building was constructed.

"Technic 1030 and 1032 are also special to me as they were the first LEGO sets I had ever seen outside of traditional toy stores. This pair of sets took Expert Builder to a whole new level. Instead of building an identifiable vehicle, you were exposed to the simple machines or mechanical principles that allowed those vehicles to operate and do what they did but in a generic format to allow for a clearer understanding of how things worked. My aunt (a civil engineer for the city of Chicago) bought me 1030 at the Museum of Science & Industry in 1983 and it has since remained in my list of favorites."

LEGO
Technic
8480
Electric System
9V
FIBER OPTIC

6285
LEGOLAND

LEGO
SYSTEM
6286

LEGOLAND
LEGO

MAKING HEADLINES

Throughout his career it has not been unusual for Adam Reed Tucker's amazing work to make mainstream media headlines. It is yet another testament to how his work has helped change people's perception and awareness of LEGO within the world of art.